MILTON PIERCE,
a professional writer who specializes in finance,
lives in New York City.

The
Four Treasures of
ALAN
SHAWN
FEINSTEIN

Milton Pierce

PRENTICE-HALL, INC.,
Englewood Cliffs, New Jersey 07632

Library of Congress Cataloging in Publication Data

Pierce, Milton.
    The four treasures of Alan Shawn Feinstein.

    Includes index.
        1. Feinstein, Alan Shawn.   2. Collectors and collecting
—United States.   3. Collectibles as an investment.
I. Title.
AM401.F35P53 1983   332.6'3 [B]   83-21265
ISBN 0-13-330481-7
ISBN 0-13-330457-4 (A Reward book : pbk.)

10 9 8 7 6 5 4 3 2 1

ISBN 0-13-330481-7

ISBN 0-13-330457-4 {A REWARD BOOK : PBK.}

Editorial/production supervision: Marlys Lehmann
Cover design © 1984 by Jeannette Jacobs
Manufacturing buyer: Pat Mahoney

This book is available at a special discount when ordered in
bulk quantities. Contact Prentice-Hall, Inc., General
Publishing Division, Special Sales, Englewood Cliffs, N.J. 07632.

Prentice-Hall International, Inc., *London*
Prentice-Hall of Australia Pty. Limited, *Sydney*
Prentice-Hall Canada Inc., *Toronto*
Prentice-Hall of India Private Limited, *New Delhi*
Prentice-Hall of Japan, Inc., *Tokyo*
Prentice-Hall of Southeast Asia Pte. Ltd., *Singapore*
Whitehall Books Limited, *Wellington, New Zealand*
Editora Prentice-Hall do Brasil Ltda., *Rio de Janeiro*

*This book is dedicated
to my children, Sam and Estee,
and to Alan's children,
Ari, Ricky, and Leila.*

Contents

Introduction:
The Legend of
Alan Shawn Feinstein

Who is Alan Shawn Feinstein?

He is considered a genius in investments and finance, but he has nothing to do with stocks or bonds. In fact, he avoids Wall Street as if it were the plague.

He is a man who publishes a newsletter that is read by thousands, and a newspaper column read by millions, yet he avoids publicity. He shuns requests for radio and television appearances and rarely goes out to public gatherings. Virtually his entire life has been spent within a 100-mile radius of a little town in Rhode Island.

His approach to high finance and economics is simple— in fact, it consists of just one basic rule. But that rule is the basis of all his success. It is the most fundamental rule of economics—the law of supply and demand.

Simply by applying this fundamental law he has amassed a fortune and has enriched the lives of countless others. The explanation is this: Alan Shawn Feinstein has discovered four areas of such profit potential that thousands of people are benefitting from them.

The four areas—Alan calls them his "treasures"—are error postage stamps, certain gemstones, demonetized bank notes, and presidential autographs. This book is about those areas—and how you can profit from them.

Do not treat this information lightly. With it, Alan Shawn Feinstein has built what has been called one of the most powerful followings in the world. His newspaper column is published across America and in many foreign nations. His newsletter, *The Insiders Report*, is read avidly in every corner of the world. People have been known to travel for thousands of miles to attend his once-a-year public seminars in Rhode Island.

This book introduces you to this man. It reveals how anyone—rich or poor—can profit from his discoveries.

1

Who Is Alan Shawn Feinstein?

I was introduced to Alan Shawn Feinstein by a headline that screamed across a full page in *The New York Times*.

YOURS FREE—My Gift To You!

As a writer of direct-mail advertising (as well as books), I knew the cost of running a full-page ad in the *Times*. I remember saying to myself, "This guy Feinstein must have a tremendous amount of confidence. He must really believe in what he's offering." I sent for that booklet.

I had heard of Alan Shawn Feinstein before. Friends had mentioned his newspaper column; they told me he was a fascinating writer. When I saw the ad and read the booklet, I knew why. His style radiated personality. He wrote to his readers and his naturalness shined through. There was something different about him. I sensed a unique person with exciting new ideas.

In the years since, I have come to know Alan Shawn Feinstein well. I now understand what sets him apart from others in his field. Perhaps the most obvious thing about him is that he sincerely cares about the people who depend on his advice. His devotion to his newsletter subscribers is unusual, and their admiration for him is legendary.

But this singular devotion to his readers is merely an expression of the man's extraordinary character. Despite his successes, he refuses to leave his beloved Rhode Island, even though he could be a celebrity in the nation's financial center. His wife has established a successful psychiatric practice in Rhode Island. It is the place where his young children are growing up. It is a place Alan Shawn Feinstein never wants to leave.

What is it that makes this man so followed, admired, and envied in every corner of the country? A man whom few people have ever seen or heard? A man who, save for his written word, shuns the limelight in the conventional areas of financial publicity everywhere?

"It's the way his writing touches people," says one admirer. He has a unique knack for showing people he really cares about them. Of course there are the unexpected extra bonuses he puts in their orders, the free scholarships he sets up for them, the money they know he gives to charity. But there is no question that his writing itself exudes a strong charisma.

Most important, it's the profit opportunities he brings to people—the same profit opportunities that you will shortly be reading about for yourself. Here is just a brief sampling of what Alan's readers have had to say about that:

> *I studied the appreciation of a few randomly selected U.S. stamps and found that some stamps had appreciated at a rate of 20 to 44 percent! I thought, "God, if I only knew then. . . ." Then I realized that this is precisely the opportunity that you are offering: the knowledge of which stamps to invest in to realize the greatest investment security and profit potential available.*
>
> D. S., Iowa

> *I called another diamond supplier and found their quote a whopping $3,000 higher. You got me a good deal!! That $3,000 you saved me paid my* Insiders Report *[subscription] up for 100 years.*
>
> J. A., Akron, Ohio

4

Alan's rise to the top of the financial world was atypical of the usual Wall Street success story. With undergraduate degrees in journalism and economics and a master's degree in education, he spent many years writing and teaching. He published a novel and several other books on the peoples of other lands, and he taught public school in New England. Yet his interest in finance and investments never waned.

Twelve years ago Alan Shawn Feinstein's newspaper column "The Treasure Chest," a collection of unique financial opportunities for the person of average means, first appeared. As his reputation grew, so did the number of newspapers that carried his column. From West Seneca, New York to McMinnville, Oregon, people were discovering Alan Shawn Feinstein.

Then Alan Shawn Feinstein made what turned out to be the most important decision of his life. This is how he related that decision to me a number of years later. "Out of the mass of material I receive and review for my newspaper column, there emerges, every so often, a really outstanding money-making opportunity. But putting it in my column, I had found out, was usually a waste, as the willy-nilly use of it by so many of the people who read it there quickly smothered its value."

That led Alan to launch a private newsletter. On November 29, 1973, the *Insiders Report* was born. It differed from his column because Alan gave his readers much more than advice. He provided them with the exact information necessary for using and profiting from his advice. "The Treasure Chest" continued to appear, but only *after* subscribers to the *Insiders Report* had a chance to put his advice to use.

Shortly thereafter, Alan's remarkable success with silver (which we detail in Chapter 2) became public knowledge. His following was growing. Newspapers in Asia, Africa, and Europe wanted his column. Soon readers of *The Economic Times, The Egyptian Gazette, The Pakistan Herald,* and *The Hong Kong Standard,* along with Americans in every state, were getting "The Treasure Chest" with their morning coffee, along with Feinstein's private newsletter, the *Insiders Report.*

Alan was still largely unknown in the canyons of Wall Street. He didn't care. He was doing what he wanted for the people he wanted to help. In fact, he has little regard for Wall Street's usual investments anyway. He never advises on stocks or bonds because he thinks they are too risky. Too many outside factors that can never be predicted can affect a security's value: The company president may embezzle a couple of million dollars; the competition may come out with a new product; soaring interest rates may drive up the cost of expansion. People get bored, scared, and angry. Who knows which emotion can adversely affect a stock next? Alan believes it's all a "crap shoot" that most people are better off without.

To say that Alan is a maverick would be a gross understatement. On January 21, 1980, he astounded the financial world with a lengthy full-page ad in *The Providence Journal and Bulletin.* In this ad he wasn't trying to persuade people to subscribe to the *Insiders Report* or to buy his books. Instead, his sole purpose was to warn every reader that gold and silver had become excessively risky investments and that now was the time to sell.

Alan spent thousands of dollars of his own money for this ad—to inform the public of the danger he saw. "It was getting ridiculous," he explains, "and it was bad for the country. People were being attracted by the soaring prices for gold and silver, paying more and more to get them because they thought gold and silver were going to go through the roof. Gold bugs were telling them gold would soon go over $1,000 an ounce. Even $2,000. Ridiculous. I decided to do something about it."

Twenty-four hours after Alan's warning appeared, the prices of gold and silver fell like meteors. Both commodities suffered the worst one-day decline in their history. Alan continued placing his full-page warnings in *The New York Times*, *The Los Angeles Times* and other major newspapers and magazines. Gold and silver continued to go down.

This unique one-man effort made Alan's name, and the value of his advice, known throughout the country. Radio stations and television news crews clamored to find out more about this mysterious wizard. They discovered what his subscribers already knew—that his main desire was to help people of average incomes make more money with less risk and to preserve the savings they had and make them grow.

If Alan Shawn Feinstein were unknown except to his subscribers, he would be perfectly satisfied. His greatest pleasure, outside his family, comes in the mail he receives each day—letters from subscribers to his *Insiders Report*, letters that display respect and admiration for a man whose advice and predictions have brought them rewards.

Alan's innovations are not limited to the advice he gives. Advertisements for his highly successful booklet *How to Make Money* told buyers to send a check dated thirty days ahead, so it couldn't be cashed until readers had a chance to decide whether they wanted to keep the book. If not, they could return it and receive their checks back. It was a unique guarantee that has since been copied many times. It may be one reason why *How to Make Money* may be the most successful 24-page financial booklet in history. It is now in its eighth printing, and has sold more than 200,000 copies!

In "The Second Treasure of Alan Shawn Feinstein," he advised readers about a number of postage stamps that he felt would dramatically increase in value. Alan was so sure of his advice that he offered another unique guarantee, believed to be another first in the annals of advertising. If the stamps he wrote about did not increase in value in one year, he would not only refund the buyers' money, he would give them a cash bonus for their time and trouble! Alan Shawn Feinstein was putting his reputation—and his money—on the line.

Since January 1981 when he first recommended those stamps, they have risen in value, up to this writing, faster than any other recommendation made by anyone else during that time.

Despite his success, Alan does not pretend to be infallible. He makes no guarantees about the advice he gives. It is something about which he constantly reminds his readers, and he urges them to carefully investigate all the opportunities he discusses. He also urges his readers to always look for the lowest possible prices on anything he recommends. Above all, Alan Shawn Feinstein possesses a degree of integrity sorely missed in today's rough-and-tumble world.

In the world of financial advice, Alan Shawn Feinstein has been:

1. First to run full-page advertisements in leading magazines and newspapers telling people about money-making opportunities and sending them information about it free so they could see it without having to send any money in advance.

2. First to ever use "live" testimonials in his literature—names and phone numbers of people throughout the country that could be called to verify the worth of this information.

3. First to offer all kinds of different items and give people exact details on how they should search in their own locales to find them at the lowest prices.

But that's not all. For years he had been contributing anonymously to people in need through churches in the Rhode Island area until one day a social worker told him about the need for food and shelter for the hungry. Since then he has given money to open Rhode Island's first day-care shelter for the homeless, as well as ten food banks to feed the needy, several of which have been named for him. Day-care centers for both the elderly and children are also named for him. He has been featured by Save the Children in *The Wall Street Journal* and *Newsweek,* and has been cited by the House of Representatives of the State of Rhode Island as one of the finest humanitarians their state has ever known. His own children were chosen to be featured on the $5 postage stamp issued by the government of Grenada commemorating the International Year of the Child.

Alan Shawn Feinstein cares about his family, about the subscribers to his newsletter, about those less fortunate than he. I am proud to be able to call him a friend; I am even prouder to be able to bring you his story.

2

A History of Success

Alan Shawn Feinstein may be to personal investment advice what the New York Yankees are to baseball—a veritable dynasty.

Since the publication of his first *Insiders Report* over ten years ago, Alan has accumulated a truly remarkable track record; a string of successes in an era when very few investments have appreciated in real value. And that doesn't even include his money-saving advice, such as his advisements to "Beware of Gold and Silver."

Alan recommends only very few of all the opportunities he examines. He carefully sifts through them all, applying his criteria of supply and demand, and chooses only the best ones to bring to his readers. The readers of the *Insiders Report* hear about his most worthwhile finds first, with explicit suggestions about what to do. The rest, of course, is up to them.

Alan's astounding string of successes began in the autumn of 1973. After thorough research, he concluded that the price of silver was far below its worth. The demand for silver was increasing, yet production was slowing down. He saw a tremendous profit potential. Now he had to decide what was the best way to profit from it.

After sorting out his options, Alan decided to purchase silver coin futures. Alan chose coins rather than pure silver because the coins, as well as their silver value, had a built-in face value that gave them added security. He purchased the right to buy ten bags of these silver coins, which sold at that time for $2,175 per bag.

The morning after his purchase, his broker called to tell him that those same bags had increased in value to $2,225 per bag—a $500 profit (on ten futures) overnight!

Three weeks after his purchase, his futures were worth $2,380 each. In three weeks Alan's gain was $205 per future—a total of $2,050.

Alan had paid only $1,000 up front for his right to those bags, a right that was *now worth $3,050.* He had more than *tripled* his money in just three weeks!

That was just the beginning. Alan had been thinking about publishing his own newsletter for some time. He wanted to wait, however, until he truly had something of value to pass along to his readers. Now he did. On November 29, 1973, in his first *Insiders Report,* Alan advised his readers: ". . . Buy Silver Now. Especially buy *silver* and *silver coin futures* if you can afford them . . . bought now, they should be worth considerably more in the months ahead. . . ."

A few days after the report went out, silver began to rise again. When it slowed its advance for some profit-taking, Alan told his readers to hold on. Silver resumed its upward climb a few days later.

Within two weeks, the price of silver went from $2.83 an ounce to $3.10. In six weeks it hit an all-time high of $4 an ounce. It continued to increase in value, hitting $6.42 an ounce shortly thereafter.

Alan's readers who bought silver futures at his urging were now able to sell them for over $30,000—with an intial investment of just $2,000—in just three months. You may have heard of someone's doubling or even tripling his money on rare occasions, but did you ever hear of anyone's advice making someone fifteen times his money in only three months?

Another of Alan's successes was in the area of diamonds. In March of 1978, readers of the *Insiders Report* were advised to purchase gem diamonds for $2,500 or less. By March of 1980, diamonds of the same size and quality were worth almost $7,000! A profit of 178 percent in two years!

Alan Shawn Feinstein's successful financial advice also extended to the field of postage stamps. In March 1979 he advised subscribers to the *Insiders Report* to buy the rare U.S. Zeppelin Stamp Set for $3,000. In one year, that set was selling for $6,750! Readers who cashed in on Alan's advice turned a profit of 125 percent in just 12 months.

What about the year 1981, when practically all collectibles, as well as precious gems, stocks, and bonds went *down* in value?

During this period Alan did not recommend investing in any of those items. Instead he searched out other unique, little-known fields where he felt his readers could make money. Two items that he did recommend collecting during that time were presidential autographs and U.S. missing-color stamps—stamps inadvertently printed by the government with one or more of their designated colors missing. These two items not only resisted the downward trend in value of practically all other collectibles, but have been soaring in value since his recommendations! In fact, since Alan Shawn Feinstein's recommendation, U.S. error stamps have been climbing in value faster than any other stamps in the world.

Alan Shawn Feinstein advised his readers to invest in the missing-color stamps in January 1981 with the following message in the *Insiders Report*.

> *If I had to choose one thing right now that I thought was going to rise in value most of all in the next few months, this would be it. I think it will be one of the most rewarding opportunities you will ever have. . . Mark my words well. This sleeping treasure is about to awake.*

It did. In the nine months after Alan's initial recommendations, U.S. error stamps skyrocketed in value. The particular stamps Alan urged his readers to buy went up an average of almost 100 percent. The proof is in the prices paid for these stamps at auctions several months after his recommendation, and the recognition by experts in this field—months after his initial recommendation—that these stamps offered the greatest potential for value in the entire stamp field. How much have his readers profited from his advice on stamps? Here are just two examples.

- Scott catalog #1355 F was worth $380 when Alan recommended it. On June 18, 1981, six months after his recommendation, it was bringing $1,500 at auctions!

- Stamp #1363 C listed at $15 in the same catalog. In August 1981, it was sold at auction for $170—almost 12 times more than its value before Alan's recommendation.

Alan's recommendation list is full of successes like these—and this just for error stamps! It would occupy too much space to list them all here, but here's a summary. Of the 55 stamps he recommended, 16 of them were bringing two to three times more than their catalog values just a few months after his recommendation, and five of them were bringing four to five times their catalog value! *Every single one of them* was higher in value than when he first recommended it. And at a time, mind you, when almost all other collectibles, including stocks, bonds, and precious gems were all going *down* in value.

This is what the March 1981 issue of *Antique and Collectors Mart* had to say about error stamps.

> . . . *U.S. errors are coming on strong with indications that the next few months may offer collectors and investors a unique opportunity. Experts are calling the error field "very much undervalued" and prices are considered to be ripe for a fast and steady takeoff. In fact, with the latest auction results, many of the errors have registered gains of up to 20% in the last two months alone.*

This article appeared two months after Alan's recommendation.

Here's what *The American Philatelic Services Report* had to say in its February–March 1981 issue under the headline "Alan Feinstein Does It Again!"

> *In what one observer has called a "masterful stroke," Alan Shawn Feinstein has again picked a big winner—possibly the biggest one of all. . . . In the past two months, certain errors have increased 20% in value and this could be just the beginning.*

The Scott Publishing Company—the most prestigious name in the entire stamp world—told its readers that it believed U.S. error stamps were the most rewarding opportunity for appreciation in the entire stamp field. This release was sent out in September 1981—a full nine months *after* Alan Shawn Feinstein's unequivocal recommendation.

Another area in which Alan Shawn Feinstein has helped his readers make money is in demonetized bank notes—bills that were printed by governments that later went out of existence or retired this currency, replacing it with a newer one. They are not only pieces of history, but works of art in their own right.

One of Alan's first recommendations of demonetized bank notes was "Japanese invasion money." Printed during World War II, it was the currency the Japanese planned to use in America if they won the war. Some people had told Alan that these bank notes were worthless and would continue to be. Alan wasn't convinced of this. He remembered what had happened during the past few years to the value of baseball cards, which for years were given away in penny packages of bubble gum. Then, as collectors became more and more interested in them, their value increased. Today, many of these baseball cards, which you could have gotten for nothing years ago, are selling for as much as $50 and $100 each.

Alan realized the value of something in limited supply with good potential appeal—especially at a time when most people *think* it is worthless, so it can be gotten at very little cost. He made his recommendations about these World War II Japanese currency bills, advising his readers where to buy them for 30 cents or less. A few months later, his readers were selling these bills for up to $5 and $10 each.

Alan's successes are not limited to the money he makes for his subscribers; he brings them information and services in many other important areas, too. Here are just a few examples from a single 12-month period:

- In August 1979, readers of the *Insiders Report* were warned about declining real estate prices in many areas—just before they began to fall.

- In October 1979 Alan established a $5,000 scholarship at Boston University for any subscriber or member of his or her family.

- In December 1979 he got his readers a huge discount on rental cars. Other discounts and free products followed.

- In June 1980, readers of the *Insiders Report* received free burglary protection. In August Alan obtained free legal advice for all his readers.

Recently, Alan's readers profited from his advice in other ways:

- He introduced his readers to an outstanding football prediction service with a money-back guarantee of satisfaction.

- He showed his readers how to profit from colored gems.

- He showed his readers the value of getting certain foreign demonetized bank notes.

- He told his readers how to help break our dependence on foreign oil.

- He showed the effect of rising gold and silver prices on inflation and why they are so dangerous to us.

- He arranged to get other valuable products free for all his readers, such as food samples, health care products, and financial guides.

- He was one of the first to advise his readers of the now-famous dental care procedure that involves the regular use of the common household ingredients: salt, baking soda, and hydrogen peroxide.

- He showed his readers exactly how to sell at a profit collectibles he had earlier advised them to get.

His versatility and his record of success set Alan apart from others in his field. Now you are going to see how *you* can profit from these characteristics yourself.

These next chapters may be the most important ones you will ever read. You will not only learn what Alan Shawn Feinstein is advising now, but how *you* can profit from his advice—right now!

3

Error Postage Stamps

A number of years ago, W. T. Robey of Washington, D.C. purchased a sheet of 100 24-cent airmail stamps from his local post office. He was not a collector; he simply needed the stamps for postage. Mr. Robey noticed that the airplane on every stamp was printed upside down. When he told the postal inspectors of his discovery, they demanded the sheet back. Ultimately, it was decided that since Mr. Robey had paid for these stamps, they were his property, not the government's.

A few years later, he sold the sheet—$24 worth of airmail stamps—for $15,000; but that was just the beginning. The last time one of these errors was sold, it went for a staggering $160,000!

Mr. Robey's case was not unique; similar finds are still being made today. In 1981 Marcia James (not her real name) of Eau Claire, Wisconsin, went to her local post office and purchased a 50-stamp sheet of the Battle of Yorktown issue. She knew immediately that one color was missing from the stamps, for which she had paid $9. So Ms. James took the sheet to a local stamp dealer and sold the set for $5,000!

Not everyone who discovers an error stamp recognizes it as such. Take the case of Robert Beck (not his real name) of Syracuse, New York. One day in 1981 Mr. Beck, a local businessman, went to the post office and was given a sheet of 50 18-cent stamps, the Edna St. Vincent Millay issue. When he returned to his store, he noticed there was no denomination on the stamps. He went back to the post office, but was told the stamps could not be returned and that he should go ahead and use them.

During the following two weeks, he mailed about 40 of the stamps, one of which was on a letter to a stamp collector. The collector spotted the error and knew the stamps might be valuable. He contacted Mr. Beck, who was glad to sell the remaining ten stamps for 18 cents each—just to get rid of them. The wise collector made a handsome profit on Mr. Beck's lack of knowledge.

Less than two months after Alan Shawn Feinstein recommended collecting color-missing stamps, many of the stamps had increased in value by 20 percent. In the next few months, many of these stamps were auctioned off at two, three, even four times their previous value. And this, Alan says, is just the beginning, for many stamp authorities now predict that missing-color error stamps have enormous appreciation potential in the coming years because of their extremely limited supply and unique appeal.

And the supply will *continue* to decrease in the years to come because demand for existing error stamps is growing and because very few new ones are being discovered. The U.S. Postal Service is very conscious of mistakes in much the same way a clothing manufacturer is; it doesn't want them to happen. When an error is found in time, the stamps are destroyed.

What you will learn in this chapter may seem different from traditional methods of stamp collecting, but forget anything you ever learned about stamps: This information can make money for you.

A missing-color error stamp is just what the name implies—one or more of the designated colors was inadvertently omitted in the printing. It happens very infrequently, but when it occurs, the mistake is quickly corrected. Few existing errors ever make it to the post office and thence to the public, but those that do could be worth a fortune some day. Presently, most are still little-known, considering their rarity, and are still available at very low prices. Larry Bustillo of the Suburban Stamp Company in Springfield, Massachusetts says the number of collectors getting into error stamps is rising. This could be very important to those who purchase these stamps for their investment value. In fact it is exactly the reason why you should buy error stamps now—and hold on to them for at least two years.

Below are some examples of the error stamps Alan is recommending.

In 1969 the upper left-hand stamp was issued to commemorate the 100th anniversary of professional baseball. Of the almost 131,000,000 stamps of this issue printed, 300 to 400 were missing the color black. This issue, with a face value of 6 cents, was recently sold at auction for $800!

In 1971 the upper right-hand stamp was issued to honor Emily Dickinson, one of this country's greatest poets. Of the more than 140,000,000 stamps printed for this issue, fewer than 250 were discovered missing both olive and black. The face value of this stamp is 8 cents; it recently sold at auction for $750! In the near future, it may be worth several times that.

The lower left-hand stamp, commemorating the Pioneer space mission, was issued in 1975. More than 173,000,000 of these stamps were made; only a few with violet-blue omitted. These 200 errors are now selling for about $900 each.

The stamp in the lower right-hand honoring Ben Franklin was issued in 1976 as part of the bicentennial series. More than 164 million were printed—1,000 were discovered lacking light blue and other colors. One 13-cent stamp recently sold for $270! Its value could increase to $1000.

These are just four of the 53 missing-color stamps recommended by Alan Shawn Feinstein. The others are listed here. These are the stamps you should attempt to acquire now, while their value is still relatively low. The beauty of buying these stamps is you can buy (and sell) them right over the phone, through recognized auctions.

Now that you know what error stamps are, where and how can you obtain them at the lowest prices?

Buying Error Stamps

At present, few dealers handle error stamps. Most are sold at auction. The two auction houses specializing in U.S. missing-color error stamps are Jacques Schiff, 195 Main Street, Ridgefield Park, NJ 07660 (201-641-5566) and Suburban Stamp Co., 1071 St. James Avenue, Springfield, MA 01101 (413-785-5348). Each holds an auction of error stamps every four or five weeks. After each auction, they issue a "price-realized" report showing what each stamp brought.

Catalog #	Year	Commemorating	Color or Type Missing	Latest Auction Price
1252	1964	American music	blue	$1,050
1271A	1965	Florida	yellow	400
1340A	1968	Hemisfair '68	white	1,400
1355A	1968	Walt Disney	ocher	370
1355D	1968	Walt Disney	black	1,250
1355F	1968	Walt Disney	blue	1,500
1362B	1968	Waterfowl conservation	red and black	1,250
1363C	1968	Christmas	light yellow	170
1370B	1969	Grandma Moses	black and blue	525
1384	1969	Christmas	red, yellow, and green	380
1414B	1970	Christmas	black	625
1414C	1970	Christmas	blue	850
1420A	1970	Pilgrims	orange and yellow	850
1444A	1971	Christmas	gold	280
1448–51B	1972	National Parks	black	700
1471A	1972	Christmas	pink	360
1473A	1972	Pharmacy	blue and orange	800
1474A	1972	Stamp collect.	black	320
1480–83B	1973	Boston Tea Party	black (engraved)	3,000
1480–83C	1973	Boston Tea Party	black (lithographed)	1,600
1488A	1973	Copernicus	orange	625
1501A	1973	Electronics	black	440
1501B	1973	Electronics	tan and lilac	420
1502A	1973	Electronics	black	625
1504A	1973	Rural America	green, red, and brown	500
1528A	1974	Horse Racing	blue	400
1538–41B	1974	Mineral heritage	Light blue, yellow	1,600

Catalog #	Year	Commemorating	Color or Type Missing	Latest Auction Price
1542	1974	Kentucky settlement	black, green, and blue	1,600
1542A	1974	Kentucky settlement	dull black	550
1547A	1974	Energy conservation	blue, orange	400
1547B	1974	Energy conservation	orange, green	675
1547C	1974	Energy conservation	green	500
1555A	1975	D. W. Griffith	brown	500
1557A	1975	Mariner 10	red	265
1557B	1975	Mariner 10	ultramarine, bistre	2,000
1560A	1975	Salem Poor	inscription on back	160
1561A	1975	Haym Salomon	inscription on back	210
1577–78	1975	Banking and commerce	brown and blue	320
1596	1975	Eagle and shield	yellow	210
1687	1976	Declaration of Independence (souv. sheet)	USA/18¢	380
1687G	1976	Declaration of Independence (ind. stamp)	USA/18¢	300
1689H	1976	Washington at Valley Forge	USA/31¢	300
1723–4	1977	Energy	dark orange	575
1800	1979	Christmas	yellow, tan, and green	650
1800	1979	Christmas	yellow and green	675
C84	1972	National parks	blue	1,050
C86A	1973	Electronics	vermillion, olive	320
C91–2	1978	Wright Brothers	black, blue	460
J89A	1979	½¢ postage due	black	380

Catalogs of upcoming auctions, plus a follow-up price-realized report, are available from both companies upon request for $1.50 each. In addition, Schiff publishes a useful booklet, "How to Bid at Auctions." Stamp-collecting publications generally mention other auction houses, which you can call to find out if they sell error stamps.

Most auction houses allow you to bid by mail or by phone prior to, or even during, the auction. If you are nearby you can attend the auctions, or you can authorize someone to bid for you. Almost any auction house can give you the names of people who specialize in bidding for others, usually for a fee of 5 percent or less.

Getting the Lowest Possible Price

When buying stamps, always look for the lowest possible price, just as you would when buying a car or suit. This is especially important because you run the risk of overbidding when you buy at auction.

How do you avoid this? Never, under any circumstances, pay more than 10 to 15 percent above the most recent auction price for *any* item. You may lose out this way, but that's better than entering a bidding war that could easily drive the price higher than its true worth.

That 10 to 15 percent ceiling protects you from being carried away. Besides, there is a 10 percent buyer's commission on the realized price that you pay to the auction house. Figure that in on top of your winning bid. The higher the selling price, the higher that commission in dollars and cents.

Are there other ways to get these stamps other than via auctions? You could advertise in stamp-collecting publications. If you attract a collector who is willing to sell you some stamps, you both avoid the 10 percent auction house commission by dealing directly. However, when these stamps come up for sale, they are generally steered to the auction houses specializing in them.

One advantage of buying through a reputable auction house is that you can be sure of the quality and authenticity of the stamp. If you ever buy through a dealer, always get a second or third opinion. Most reputable dealers will let you purchase a stamp on approval. If another stamp expert doubts its worth, you can get your money back. As mentioned earlier, however, most dealers do not sell error stamps because of their rarity and the relative newness of the field. But that may change as error stamps become more well known and as their values increase.

The Condition
of Error Stamps

You don't have to be too preoccupied with the condition of error stamps, according to Larry Bustillo. "Since most of them are modern issues," he says, "99 percent are well centered and never hinged. They have not had the time to acquire tears, wrinkles, and creases."

Waiting for Your Stamps
to Appreciate in Value

Don't buy *any* stamps and expect to make a quick profit on them in a month or two. You might, but generally you have to plan to hold your stamps at least a year or two. Remember, trends indicate error stamps have a long, profitable future ahead. People who profit the most will likely be those who hold on to their stamps the longest.

Caring for
Your Error Stamps

Be very careful to keep your error stamps away from water and humidity. Never put them in your pocket. Take care not to wrinkle or damage them. Remember, a damaged error stamp is worth less than those in mint condition, and may even be worthless. Never hinge them in an album, and avoid containers of poly-vinyl chloride (PVC).

Selling Your Error Stamps

Before you make a final decision to sell your error stamps, get the latest realized prices from a number of auction houses that specialize in them to give you an idea of what your stamps are worth.

You can sell the stamps through the same house you bought them from and you don't have to be present; you can mail the stamps to the auction house. Just make sure you package them well, send them via registered mail, and insure them for their value.

Before issuing your consignment agreement, talk to the auctioneer. Make sure there aren't a large number of similar stamps being offered at that particular auction. You should also establish a minimum bid or reserve you will accept for your stamps. Remember, you will have to pay most auction houses a 10 percent seller's fee, so figure that into your minimum bid.

Other Sales Avenues

With more and more collectors asking dealers to be on the lookout for error stamps, you might very well get lucky if you call some of the dealers in your area. Don't be surprised, however, if their interest is minimal. As explained earlier, this field is so new most dealers may not have any clientele for these stamps, so they do not deal in them.

Another route for selling error stamps is through leading stamp magazines, such as *Linn's Stamp News,* the largest in the field. You can place classified ads asking for the "best offer," then wait for the returns to come in. If you think you can get a better price at auction, hold off to sell them there.

A Final Word on Error Stamps

At the present time, there is almost no other financial opportunity with the profit potential of error stamps. The supply is limited, the demand is growing, and prices are currently considered undervalued. Although no guarantees can be made, of course, the profit potential in this field is outstanding.

In fact, because of the new growing interest in this field, a stamp club especially for U.S. error stamp collectors has just started. It puts out a monthly report telling all the news about these error stamps and how you can best profit from them.

Readers of this book can get a free copy of the latest issue of the newsletter by writing to U.S. Error Stamp Club Newsletter, P.O. Box 645, Wilmington, MA 01887.

Here is a list of other stamp publications you can write to obtain a free copy.

Linn's Stamp News
P.O. Box 29
Sidney, OH 45367

Stamp Trade International
1839 Palmer Avenue
Larchmont, NY 10538

Stamp Collector
Box 706
Albany, OR 97321

Mekeel's Weekly Stamp News
Box 1660
Portland, ME 04104

Strickly U.S.
Dunedin, FL 33528

The Stamper
3230 West 194th Street
Homewood, IL 60430

Scott Stamp Market Update
Three East 57th Street
New York, NY 10022

American Philatelic Services Report
Box 57
Lewiston, NY 14092

Here is how you can profit from this field:

1. Send for free sample copies of any of the foregoing publications you want to get. Be sure to get the latest copy of the U.S. Error Stamp Club newsletter.

2. Call or write for the latest Schiff and Suburban auction catalogs, or any other auctions you may know or discover.

3. When you get their catalogs, circle any of the issues recommended in this chapter.

4. Right before the auction, call to place your bids on the stamps you want. The auctioneers will tell you if they already have any higher bids, so you can adjust yours accordingly if you wish.

5. If you can get any of these stamps anywhere else at less cost than they are selling for at auction (from dealers or collectors who are willing to take a little less for a quick sale), by all means do so.

6. Watch the stamp newspapers for upcoming publicity in this field and the stamp auctions for their latest prices. Better still, just put away those you get for a year or two and then check their latest prices. You may be overjoyed at what you find.

Ten Tips
for Buying Stamps

1. Always buy your stamps in mint to very fine—never hinged—condition. (Stamps should be ultraclean with nothing attached to them.) Stamps in this condition will appreciate in value the fastest.

2. Do not buy "cheap" stamps. If you can get five stamps for $100 apiece or one stamp for $500, always purchase the more expensive stamp. Don't waste your time with stamps that will never be rare.

3. Buy stamps that have a proven record of popularity. You can gauge this popularity by checking older catalogues and realized auction prices.

4. Shop around for the best possible price.

5. Become informed by reading stamp publications and by talking with dealers and other experts in the field.

6. Buy at retail, but be prepared to sell at wholesale. Dealers, unless they have a client who wants a specific stamp, will never pay you the retail price. Of course, they will *sell* the same stamp for the retail price.

7. Be patient—in buying stamps as well as in waiting for them to appreciate in value.

8. Protect your stamps. Keep them in a safety deposit box and be very careful when handling them.

9. Get to know the catalog classifications of stamps. Every stamp has a universal catalogue number, and many people refer to the numbers when talking about them.

10. Don't be afraid to enjoy your new opportunity. Every financial opportunity has its own risks, but don't be afraid to take chances. The odds here are on your side.

4

The Lure of Gems

The lure of gems has been with us as long as records have been kept. What makes gems so popular? One reason has been their increasing value over the years. Throughout history, gemstones have proven to be an excellent investment, and in recent times they have been valuable hedges against inflation. From 1971 to 1978, for example, gemstones as a group appreciated in value about 25 percent annually. Certain gems went up much more.

Here's what one expert says about colored gems:

> After centuries as a favored store of value for the wealthy in Europe and the Far East, many colored gems are now demonstrating investment luster in the U.S. Prices for fine rubies, sapphires, and emeralds, to name the best-known colored gems, have doubled during the past three years, while pink tourmaline, red spinel, aquamarine, and precious topaz have appreciated sharply in recent months. All over the globe, indeed, demand for colored gems is growing.

Enhancing their appeal is the fact that colored gems aren't vulnerable to exchange controls, eminent domain, zoning, changing neighborhoods, or confiscatory taxes. With the main basis of value in gems being rarity, and colored gems being

40 times more rare than diamonds, you can see their future appreciation potential.

An alternative to the most obvious colored gems—rubies, sapphires, and emeralds—are the so-called semiprecious gems. That's a term, by the way, that many people in the trade disavow, because some of these gems are actually rarer than rubies, sapphires, and emeralds and can be very expensive. But many others are both rare and relatively *inexpensive*.

Top-grade aquamarines currently go for about $600 a carat, cat's eyes for roughly $2,500, green garnets for around $1,200, peridots for $200, tanzanites for $1,200, imperial topazes for about $600, and pink tourmalines for $200.

A top-grade, one-carat ruby is worth perhaps $5,000 or $6,000 a carat. A sapphire, about $3000 a carat. A one-carat emerald, over $10,000. Prices skyrocket with size. Thus, a four-carat ruby of the finest quality fetches $25,000 per carat. No mystery why, either: At any given time, only two or three will be up for sale.

"Under the circumstances, a number of experts advise gem bugs to concentrate on medium-grade rubies, sapphires, and emeralds," says a former gemologist with the Smithsonian Institution and the author of four books on colored stones. "The very top-grade gems aren't the only ones that have appreciated. To me, saying only the top grades are good is like saying the only good real estate is beach-front property. I think if you buy attractive medium-grade gems at a reasonable price from a reputable source, you stand an excellent chance of increasing the value of your assets."

Is there any danger that gem prices will stop going up? Not in the foreseeable future, the experts seem to agree. "I'm recommending to my clients investing in good quality color stones because they are difficult to find and will increase in value," says Nathalie Hocq, director of design for Cartier in Paris.

Alan Shawn Feinstein goes one step further. "Buy the rarest gems available," he says. "The rarer, the better."

What's Ahead

Knowledgeable people in this field, aside from Alan Shawn Feinstein, believe that colored gems will continue to increase in value at least as much as inflation and some gems much more. Here are some reasons why:

Colored gemstones cannot be found now in sufficient amounts to satisfy present demands. Certain high-quality stones, such as large, top-color rubies, are already almost impossible to get.

Even when—and perhaps especially when—the current recession ends, inflation and its related problems seem certain to continue. Therefore, it will take more money to buy gemstones even if demand remains static. But demand is *not* remaining static. It is growing. More and more of these gemstones are being sought after as discreet and portable wealth.

Americans, usually the last to catch on in such areas, are now beginning to awaken to the true value of these gems. When this happened with diamonds and gold, prices skyrocketed. The mechanism for marketing colored gemstones in the United States has already been created and will soon be under way in full force, creating millions of dollars of extra sales of these gems.

Even the jewelry industry, as evidenced in its trade publications, is awakening to the increasing investment potential of gems.

Present mines, most of which have been worked for thousands of years, are yielding far fewer gems now. Many of these fields are already completely exhausted, and new gem fields are not being found in sufficient numbers to replace them.

Current hand-tool mining methods are insufficient to satisfy demand, and their production cannot be sufficiently increased. High-volume mining methods have been curbed due to environmental considerations.

In many areas that are major sources of gems, the political situation is precarious. This factor has already caused the supply to decrease, since many dealers are now holding on to their fine colored gems to use as portable emergency bank accounts.

Many fine colored gemstones are *much* rarer than corresponding diamonds. Because of the lesser publicity and marketing emphasis on them, they are available for less. That situation may soon be a thing of the past, though. Some leading financial advisors—aside from Alan Shawn Feinstein—agree that the appreciation in colored gemstones could be tremendous.

The table below shows the range of current prices for precious stones and gems. If the current trend holds true, in ten years the value of these gems could be more than four times today's prices.

ESTIMATED WHOLESALE PRICES FOR PRECIOUS GEMS
AND STONES, PER CARAT:
(Note the wide range of prices, depending on quality.)

Carats	Emerald	Ruby	Sapphire
1	$250 to $14,000	$300 to $6500	$150 to $3000
3	$650 to $25,000	$800 to $15,000	$300 to $9,000
5	$750 to $28,000	$1000 to $18,000	$400 to $11,000

Not only are gems becoming more popular, they are also becoming more scarce; fewer gem deposits are being discovered. Another consideration is that gem-rich countries (such as Thailand, Burma, and South Africa) are likely to limit or curtail their gem output.

And of course, gems are, in a word, beautiful. Many gem owners treasure them for their exquisitely radiant luster alone. Their beauty is thus also a cause of their increasing popularity.

The ABCs of Gems

With few exceptions, gems are minerals. Exceptions are jet and amber which originate from living vegetation and tree sap; and coral and pearls, which are secreted by animal organisms.

In the past, gems were classified as either precious or semiprecious. Precious gems included diamonds, rubies, emeralds, and sapphires; all others were classified as semiprecious. This distinction has now been generally discontinued because many of the so-called semiprecious gems are now fashionable, beautiful, and expensive.

It is the job of the gemcutter or lapidary to bring out the inherent beauty of the gem; to cut, polish, and shape it.

The one common physical property all gems possess is hardness. The Mohs scale categorizes the hardness of selected common minerals. The hardest mineral, with a grade of ten, is the diamond. The softest mineral, talc, has a grade of one. The following table shows degrees of hardness for minerals and gems:

1. Talc	7. Quartz
2. Gypsum	7½–8. Emerald
3. Calcite	8. Topax
4. Fluorite	9. Corundum, Sapphire
5. Apatite	and Ruby
6. Feldspar	10. Diamond

Gemcutters will not consider anything less than a seven to be a gem.

What makes a gem particularly appealing is its color. The interaction of light upon the gem also enhances its beauty. An opaque gem like jasper, for instance, produces a cat's-eye effect when light is shone upon it. In purchasing a gem, choose one whose color appeals to you. Base your decision also on how much it will bring when you decide to sell it.

When light passes through a stone, it is said to be transparent. Topaz and amethyst are examples of transparent gems. Stones such as these should be cut, polished, and positioned so they reflect light. This procedure is called faceting, and the polished gem faces are called facets.

Synthetic stones have been produced in laboratories and commercially. For a gem to be considered synthetic, its chemical and structural properties must be identical to the real thing. Synthetic emeralds, rubies, sapphires, and spinels are already produced commercially. Synthetic gems pose a threat to gem dealers because they are difficult to distinguish from the real thing.

Precious and Semiprecious Stones

The *major* distinction between precious and semiprecious stones is that precious stones are currently more valuable. A wise investor, however, should consider both, says Alan Shawn Feinstein, because most semiprecious stones offer another advantage in addition to being beautiful and scarce—they are, at present, inexpensive. An investment in some well-chosen semiprecious gems could be very worthwhile.

Here are a few examples of the kinds of semiprecious gems Alan advises you to look into: aquamarine, imperial topaz, tourmaline, spinel, tsavorite, and amethyst.

How to Buy Gems

When evaluating a gem, keep in mind that the value is determined by cut, carat, clarity, and color.

View the gem under magnification to determine the

quality of cut and polishing. Awkward angles of cutting affect the reflection of light and brilliance, and therefore the value. Also, check for any imperfections.

When examining gems, color is perhaps your most important consideration. The exact shade of red in rubies and green in emeralds will determine, to a great extent, the value of the stone. Color grading in gems, however, is not as well-defined as it is for diamonds. It is, therefore, very important to deal with a reputable gem firm known for first-rate technical expertise. Whenever you're thinking of purchasing gems, never do so without first consulting an experienced, independent appraiser. This is your best means of avoiding a rip-off.

Before it reaches the jewelry store, a gem goes through a series of transformations. The miner usually uncovers a very rough stone. The cutter molds the stone into an artistic shape. The wholesaler then receives the stone and sells it to a dealer, who, in turn, casts it into jewelry before resale.

Through each process, the value of the gem increases. It thus follows that the closer you get to the original source, the less expensive the stone will be. Therefore, when buying gems for investment, try to purchase them at the wholesale level.

Always purchase top-quality stones—whether it's a semiprecious stone at $100 to $500 a carat or a precious gem at $10,000 a carat or more. In any case, the key to a good investment is: Buy the best of whatever you buy. The best is what will appreciate in value the most.

The crème de la crème of semiprecious stones includes very fine topaz, tourmaline, and peridot. All these could increase tremendously in value in coming years, says Alan Shawn Feinstein. One colored gem, precious topaz, might be a particular winner, since it is found only at a few mine sites in Brazil.

Those topazes that are of three carats or more that are a fine gold color, or those with some pink or strawberry in them, are considered even rarer and could increase substantially in value.

One final note: There's one more important factor to consider before purchasing gems. Never buy one that is not aesthetically pleasing to you. Buy a gem you enjoy having and its value to you will be twofold.

Selling Your Gems

The first step in selling your gemstones is to get a trustworthy appraisal of their fair market value. (Usually you should check the appreciation every two or three years.) Always look for an independent accredited gemologist to appraise your gems. After they have been appraised, you may want to show them to neighbors and friends. Many people have sold their collections at a profit through word-of-mouth and through ads in newspapers. Another means is through the advice or contacts of the person you purchased them from.

When you purchase any gems, discuss your selling expectations with the seller. This way you will know how helpful he or she will be when the time comes for you to sell. You should plan to keep any gem you buy for at least three years. In the field of gems, patience goes a long way toward helping you achieve a great financial reward. Besides, you can enjoy the beauty of your purchase as long as you own it—no small pleasure indeed.

You can get a good publication in this field free by mentioning this book. It is the *House of Onyx* newsletter, One Main Street, Greenville, KY 42345.

Your local library should have other publications on colored gems, tracing their history, rarity, and even their potential for increased value. Many of these publications and books will have colored plates of these gems as well, showing their true color brilliance.

How You Can Profit
from This Field

1. Send for free information such as the *House of Onyx* newsletter.

2. Visit your local library for the most popular books and any recent articles on colored gems.

3. Read these and see which gems appeal to you most.

4. Find a reputable financial advisor or wholesaler of colored stones who will agree to represent you (for a small fee, of course).

5. Before buying, discuss with your representative your exact needs, how long you wish to hold the stones, and how you can sell them. Be sure your representative can satisfy you in his or her ability to help you sell your gems when the time comes.

6. Buy only what you personally like, and plan to hold your gems for at least three or four years.

7. Beautiful precious gems are one of the few things in the world you can buy both for enjoyment and for appreciation potential. Take advantage of this. Whatever you get, buy it first because you love having it—says Alan Shawn Feinstein. Then any appreciation you realize in years to come will be an added plus.

Four Tips on Buying Gems

1. Buy only medium- to top-quality gems for investment. The majority of stones that reach this country are considered "commercial" and are used to manufacture low-cost jewelry. A smaller number are of medium- to top-grade quality, and an even smaller number are considered top quality.

2. Rubies may be the best value at present because of their appreciation potential. New emerald mines are being discovered. Diamonds, although almost certain to increase in value, will never be rare. Rubies are scarce, however, and are becoming scarcer. New finds are being made, but most are not investment quality. Sapphires, although still priced below rubies, emeralds, and diamonds, are in very stable supply. Since most sapphires come from Australia, the number available should remain consistent.

3. Color is the most important asset to the future value of a gem. There are not yet any specific standards for certifying gems (except for diamonds). Color, however, cannot be disputed.

4. Attempt to buy gems at wholesale. Stones become much more expensive at the retail level.

5

Demonetized Bank Notes

In the early days of World War II, the Japanese were ecstatic over their great military successes against the United States. Confident of a complete, final victory over the Americans, they actually made a formal agreement with Germany to divide the United States between them.

The currency pictured on page 53—printed by the Japanese and redeemable in U.S. dollars—was being used by their forces in occupied Malaya. It was reportedly the same kind of money the Japanese planned to use here in the United States when their conquest was complete.

Of course, the Japanese victory never materialized, and after the war most of these bank notes were destroyed. Recently, however, a large cache of them was discovered stored in a warehouse. All were in perfect, mint condition, just as they had come off the Japanese presses 40 years ago.

Alan Shawn Feinstein reported this discovery to his readers. He told them of the unique appeal and potential appreciation value of these historical keepsakes. He told them where they could get these unusual bills for just a few cents apiece. Here is a typical letter he received from one of his readers just a few weeks later.

In June I bought one thousand $10 bank notes from you for 30 cents each. Since that time, I have sold a number of them for $5 each. When I opened your letter today one chap in my office offered me $30 for 10. . . . For this tremendous return on my investment even at the $3 apiece sale (which is the cheapest I've sold them at) I'm making 10 times my investment. . . .

A very happy
subscriber, G. G.

A short while after Alan broke the news about this bank note, an advertisement appeared in a national publication offering these same bank notes for many times their low cost:

Since that first discovery Alan has uncovered several other demonetized bank notes throughout the world with interesting appeal. All are available at very low prices.

"Demonetized" means they are no longer legal currency. In most cases no more will ever be made. The number of bills remaining is constantly shrinking.

These demonetized bank notes are works of art as well as pieces of history. Unique treasures from another era, they are beautiful, exciting, and becoming scarcer and more valuable all the time. Following are descriptions of the ones Alan has selected.

Argentine 50-Peso Bill

This 50-peso note depicts the famous Argentine general San Martin. A victim of ravaging inflation, this bill was taken out of circulation in 1978.

Biafran One-Pound Bill

This money comes from the ill-fated African Republic whose people were crushed in their effort to break away from Nigeria. This one-pound note, no longer in circulation, is a reminder of those who gave their lives for their independence.

Bulgarian 50-Leva Note

From behind the Iron Curtain comes this bill, one of a seven-note set, multicolored and watermarked. The Communist leadership of Bulgaria has announced that no more of these bills will be allowed out of the country. The set is a true collector's item.

Burmese Ten-Rupee Bill

This bank note is one of two issued by the Japanese during their occupation of Burma during World War II; they were used by the Burmese until they were liberated by the Allies in 1945. This money is considered the most beautiful of the Japanese invasion money.

Chilean 5,000-Escudo Bill

This bill, depicting the famed Chilean revolutionary Jose Marquiel Carrera, was recently withdrawn from circulation. Also a victim of runaway South American inflation, it was first printed in 1973. Now that Chile's monetary system is based on the peso, no more escudos will ever be printed.

Indonesian 50-Sen Bill

This bill was used as Indonesian currency more than two decades ago. Once plentiful, it is now rapidly becoming scarce.

Indonesian 2½-Rupiah Bill

This is one of a set of 19 beautiful multicolored Indonesian bank notes. Taken out of circulation because of staggering inflation, they will never be printed again. The set includes the 50-sen note mentioned previously, as well as four smaller sen notes.

Laotian One-Kip Bill

This is one of four bills from Laos issued before the war in Indochina spread and brought the Communists to power. These lovely bank notes, a collector's dream from days gone by, will never be printed again.

Mongolian 25-Tugrik Bill

This bill is one of a set of three high-value bank notes from the land of Mongolia. They bear a vignette of the Mongol horsemen—the descendants of Genghis Khan and his ravaging hordes who swept through Asia early in the 13th century.

Paraguayan One-Guarani Bill

This bill was used in the 1950s in Paraguay, where men from all over the world met to spy and plot. Taken out of circulation by the military dictatorship which now runs the country, it is a rare memento.

Philippine Ten-Peso Bill

This is more Japanese invasion money, used in the Philippines during the Japanese occupation of World War II. After the war ended, the Filipinos destroyed most of these bills—their way of destroying painful memories—but many were kept as souvenirs, a tribute to the courageous foes of the Axis powers during WWII.

Philippine Guerrilla Bill

This money, also from the Philippines, was issued by the Filipino insurgents during World War II in open defiance of the Japanese occupation. Being captured with this money often meant death at the hands of the Japanese.

Uruguayan 100-Peso Bill

This one of a set of four bills used in the mid-1900s during the tyrannical reign of Tuparmaros. It also became a victim of typical South American inflation and is today a valuable collector's item.

But perhaps the most famous note of all is Great Britain's ten-shilling cancelled military currency note from World War II. Formerly considered to be exceptionally rare, 100,000 of them were unexpectedly found in British government vaults. British military currency has always been highly prized by collectors everywhere, but, although the British government had promised that no more of these particular notes would ever be made, the fact that such a quantity was now about to enter the market threatened to depress their value sharply.

To protect their value, Alan Shawn Feinstein purchased the entire stock, offered some of them to his readers, and then, in the presence of a police investigator and a certified public accountant, destroyed the surplus so as to protect the value of the notes that readers had bought. Within a matter of weeks these notes had so appreciated in value that their owners could begin selling them off at a good profit. Alan had not merely *shown* his readers a profit opportunity; in effect, he had *created* one.

These unique collector's items are presently available at low prices. And every December, Alan Shawn Feinstein apprises his readers on their current prices—so they can see exactly what happens to the value of these bank notes year after year. Here are their current retail values.

ASF Recommended *Bank Notes* *(with their catalog numbers)*	*Current Retail* *Value*
ARGENTINE 50-Peso (301)	$ 1.75
BIAFRAN 1-Pound (5)	2.00
BRITISH 10-Shilling (m 35)	200.00

BULGARIAN 7-pc set (81–87)	4.00
BURMESE 10-Rupee (11b)	1.50
BURMESE 100-Rupee (12b)	2.00
CHILEAN 5000 Escudo (114)	4.75
INDONESIAN 50-Sen (94)	1.00
LAOTIAN 1-KIP (2)	1.50
LAOTIAN 4 pc set (2, 20, 21, 22)	6.00
MALAYAN $10.00 (24)	4.00
MALAYAN $100.00 (25)	8.75
MONGOLIAN 3-pc. set (32, 33, 34)	130.00
PARAGUAYAN 1-Guarani (102a)	1.75
PHILIPPINE 10-Peso (110 or 111)	1.00
PHILIPPINE 100-Peso (112)	2.00
PHILIPPINE GUERRILLA	3.00
URUGUAYAN 4-pc. set (47, 50, 52, 53)	45.00
URUGUAYAN 5000-Peso Overprint (57)	12.00

All the above retail prices are for these bills in mint, uncirculated condition, except for the Philippine and Burmese bills, which are in circulated condition.

As you can see, the prices of these bank notes are generally quite low. The supply is limited. They have artistic and historic value. It all adds up to exciting potential profits if you are willing to hold on to these bills a while.

You should be able to get these at wholesale prices up to 50 percent or even more off retail prices from wholesale dealers throughout the country.

Buying Demonetized Bank Notes

Ask the owner of your local coin store if he knows of a wholesale bank note dealer. Or you can write to the Educational Coin & Bank Note Company, Box 3826, Kingston, NY 12401, which has the largest supply of bank notes in the world. Also, Alan

Shawn Feinstein publishes a wholesale price list showing the latest wholesale prices at which you should be able to get these. For a free copy of the latest issue write: P. O. Box 2065B, Cranston, RI 02905.

As stated previously, you should be able to get these bank notes at substantially less than their retail prices. First get the latest free wholesale price list, then check the classified ad section of such publications as *The Coin Wholesaler* (100 Bailey St. Rossville, GA 30741), *Coin World* (P.O. Box 150, Sidney, OH 45367), or *World Coin News* (Iola, WI 54990). Many bank note dealers advertise in these. You can even place want ads that may attract other wholesalers or even collectors who may be willing to sell.

Banks and foreign monetary outlets may also be sources worth checking. Remember, these are demonetized bank notes, and are no longer legal currency. Their value is as collector's items.

You should also know about the three major references in this field: The Pick *Standard Catalog of World Paper Money,* Krause Publications, Iola, WI 54990, $35. This gigantic book lists almost all the world's bank notes—many thousands. However, it comes out only every three or four years, and the prices may not reflect current market values. The second publication, which deals with generally inexpensive banknotes—those under $50.00—is *The Collectors Guide and Catalog of World Paper Money,* Box 3826, Kingston, NY 12401. Price: $8.50. The other publication is *The Vanishing Treasure,* which deals exclusively with the bank notes selected by Alan Shawn Feinstein. *The Vanishing Treasure* is published and updated every year. If you are interested in only those specific bank notes, write: Alan Shawn Feinstein & Associates, P. O. Box 2065B, Cranston, RI 04905. The price is $10.

Conditions of Bank Notes

As with stamps, the condition of bank notes is an important factor in determining their present and potential value. Uncirculated bank notes are generally more valuable than circulated ones.

There are seven condition grades of paper money:

Crisp Uncirculated. The note is perfectly preserved and shows no indication of circulation or mishandling.

Extremely Fine. The note is of nearly uncirculated quality, exhibiting only the slightest evidence of wear.

Very Fine. The note is undamaged but shows substantial signs of wear, possibly including multiple folds, slight wrinkles, or even traces of dirt.

Fine. The note exhibits substantial evidence of circulation, feels somewhat limp, and may have substantial surface dirt, many folds, creases, or wrinkles, and, in some cases, small tears along the edges.

Very Good. The note has obvious damage, including strong tears, missing portions of the margins or corners and/or heavy soiling.

Good. The note is badly damaged, with tears extending along the creases and well into the printed design, although no part of the printed design is missing.

Poor. The note is severely damaged in all respects and may be torn so badly a portion of the design is missing.

Although these guidelines are somewhat less strict than those for stamps and coins, condition is very important. Whenever possible, attempt to acquire bank notes in uncirculated condition. If you find, after checking a few sources, that these bank notes are not available in uncirculated condition, work your way down the ladder. However, once you reach *good*, do not consider purchasing them. The future of bank notes in fine or lesser condition is severely restricted.

One advantage you have in dealing with demonetized bank notes, especially the ones selected by Alan Shawn Feinstein, is that counterfeiting is almost nonexistent. At present, the resale values are too slight to attract counterfeiters. However, the possibility is one you should be aware of. Unless you get a guarantee of genuineness from a trusted source, always get a second or third opinion on anything you purchase and a 30-day, money-back guarantee. In case it turns out to be not as it was represented, you can return it.

Another advantage of Alan's selected bank notes is that they are available in good quantities and are widely dispersed throughout the country.

Caring for Your Bank Notes

Paper is subject to many conditions that cause it to deteriorate. There are ways to protect your bank notes from damage and a subsequent depreciation in value:

1. Keep them in a dry, cool place, away from sources of heat and humidity.

2. Keep them out of direct sunlight and strong artificial light. Both will cause bank notes to fade.

3. Keep them in glassine or mylar envelopes that can be purchased in any stamp or hobby store.

4. Handle them only with tweezers or stamp tongs. Don't hold them by the corners and don't smoke, eat, or drink while handling them.

Selling Your
Bank Notes for a Profit

As mentioned earlier, you should retain your bank notes for at least a few years to get a good return on them. With current prices so very low, you can afford to buy in large quantities and hold them for future resale, perhaps a few at a time. You may, however, wish to keep them as permanent historical collections, as many people are doing.

Here are ways to resell:

1. Often you can sell to dealers. Make sure, however, that you are fully aware of current prices and market conditions before attempting this. Call two or three dealers and ask the selling prices of bank notes you want to sell. Then you can base *your* selling price on their offers. However, realize that dealers only buy items they want to sell and usually only offer well under their own selling prices. If it's something they don't want, they won't offer anything for it. Never try to sell to a dealer if he doesn't want them, and don't be discouraged if dealers don't want these yet. They're in business to make money, and these inexpensive bank notes may not yet be profitable for them to sell.

2. Interest your neighbors and friends in this field. Show them your collection and offer to get them some if they're interested. Many people have started businesses for themselves this way.

3. Auctions of bank notes are becoming more frequent as this field expands. See the newspapers listed previously, in which auctions are advertised regularly.

4. Flea markets and collectors' clubs are two other sales avenues. Even if they're not presently dealing in bank notes, why not awaken their interest? Paper money is a perfect companion hobby for stamp, coin, and autograph collectors.

Prices are not yet prohibitive to small collectors, but that may not last for long, especially if the rapidly increasing value of baseball cards is any indication. Baseball cards have risen rapidly in value for the past few years. Why don't we recommend those? Because prices have *already* reached a very high level—too high to offer any good near-term price appreciation.

Bank notes, however, are another story. They are still very low in price, still a ground-floor opportunity, and they give you historical worth and beautiful artwork. Plus that great feature—limited supply and growing demand. Most important, most people think they're worthless. When most people don't know about something or think it's practically worthless, *that's* the time you can get it at a "practically worthless" price.

Bank Notes:
More than Just
a Financial Opportunity

We, of course, want you to profit from this field. But you should also appreciate bank notes for their historic and artistic value. When you take one of these in your hand and feel the texture, study the design, and think about its historic implications, you may find yourself appreciating it in a way that can't be explained in words.

You might even find yourself becoming an enthusiastic fan, a real live collector. This might make you want to hold on to your bank notes longer than you ever expected when you got them—which may not be a bad idea. Not only would you enjoy the pleasure and satisfaction of collecting something you truly like, but collectors have usually found that the longer you hold on to something, the better the chances are that you will realize a higher profit when you sell.

You have time working for you—ironing out all the economic hills and valleys—ever marching on, working towards increasing the long-term value of any and all items with historic value and an ever-shrinking supply. The ones who hold on to these paper treasures the longest could well find themselves reaping the greatest profits of all.

The Experiment

In 1981 Alan Shawn Feinstein called together his three children—Ari, 14, Ricky, 12, and Leila, 9—and told them about: colored gems, error stamps, and bank notes.

"Remember," he said, "the gems are the most beautiful, the stamps have the best current resale market, and the bank notes are the most unknown and least expensive. Which one would you choose?"

Ari chose the stamps, Ricky chose the gems, and Leila chose the bank notes. Each got a small portfolio of their choice to put away toward their future education.

A few years from now, which one will prove most fortunate with his or her choice? Nobody knows, but each stands a great chance of reaping a sizable windfall from his or her decision. And so will you if you pick any one of these fields that appeals to you, study it, and buy wisely. Then let time work for you.

6

Presidential Autographs

Does the following letter seem strange to you? It's how one man built a substantial collection of signatures from famous people. One of his responses, from President Ronald Reagan, recently sold for $2,800!

> *Dear Senator _____:*
>
> *My wife Jane is pregnant with our first child. I have been an admirer of yours for many years and plan to name the child after you. If it isn't too much trouble, I would appreciate your writing a letter to our unborn child, with some advice that our child might be able to follow. My wife and I would truly appreciate this.*
>
> *Sincerely,*

Many people are making huge profits from presidential autographs. Here is another example.

When Richard Nixon resigned from the presidency in August 1974, he signed a letter of resignation as a matter of protocol. For the next few years, it was believed that this was the only resignation letter that existed. It wasn't.

Another resignation letter appeared on the market, with

some authorities speculating that Nixon unsuspectingly signed the duplicate. In January 1981, Alan Shawn Feinstein heard that the duplicate was to be auctioned off in New York. He went to New York and bought that letter for $6,250.

One week later, he received a call from the president of a New York travel agency, acting on behalf of an anonymous client. Alan was offered $10,000 for that letter. That was a fast profit of $3,750—in one week!

America is well over 200 years old, yet only 39 men have held the highest office in the United States. From George Washington to Ronald Reagan, presidential signatures are a living testimony of American history. These signatures are in very limited supply—particularly those of 18th- and 19th-century presidents—yet they are extremely undervalued. That situation is beginning to change, however, as more and more national magazines report on the significance and value of these autographs.

To our knowledge, presidential autographs have seldom decreased in value—even during times of tight money—and anything that holds its value so well in tight times is a likely candidate for appreciation whenever the monetary climate improves.

"They are underpriced and have a long way to go to catch up with other collectibles," says Lee Simonson of American Collectibles. "As an example, the highest-priced presidential autograph sold to date was an autographed letter by George Washington which went for $55,000. (By comparison, the highest priced coin went for $1.5 million, oil paintings for several million.)"

"Autographs are being acquired as investments by some pension and profit-sharing plans," wrote John W. Hazard in the June 8, 1981 *U.S. News and World Report*. "Appraisers say that autographs are underpriced compared with paintings, stamps, and other collectibles."

This is the conclusion Alan Shawn Feinstein has reached as well. He felt autographs, especially presidential ones, had great profit potential—and with his purchase of the Nixon letter, he began to prove it.

Starting a Presidential Autograph Collection

The beauty of collecting presidential autographs is that you can begin wherever you like. If you have a favorite president, you might want to concentrate on collecting his signatures and memorabilia alone. Or you could try to collect some memorabilia from each of our 39 presidents.

You might wish to concentrate on handwritten, signed letters (which are quite expensive), or on dictated or typed letters signed by the president, or on signed pictures, checks or other documents. Whatever you choose will make for an interesting, rewarding opportunity.

Although autographed letters (ALS) have the most value, don't overlook clipped signatures or cancelled checks. Of clipped signatures, Lee Simonson says, "They are an inexpensive way to collect presidential signatures and they are becoming scarce."

Many clipped signatures can be purchased for less than $200, particularly those of presidents Arthur, Grant, Pierce, and Buchanan. Sixty dollars will get you a clipped signature of Rutherford B. Hayes.

Not all clipped signatures are inexpensive, however. An Abraham Lincoln clipped signature, one of the more popular autographs among collectors, sells for $750.

You should be familiar with autograph jargon. ALS means a handwritten, signed letter. LS or TLS means a dictated or typed signed letter. DS is a signed document, check, or picture. Incidentally, in autograph jargon, a collector is a *philographer*.

When you consider signed letters, content is an important factor. "A handwritten letter from Harry Truman talking about the weather," says Simonson, "is less valuable than an order he may have signed to drop the atomic bomb."

The Rarest of the Rare

For each type of autograph, some signatures are rarer than others. The rarest handwritten letters (ALS) are those of Presidents Eisenhower, Hoover, Andrew Johnson, Kennedy, and Polk. The rarest cancelled checks are those of 19th-century presidents Buchanan, Pierce, and Tyler. They sell for $5,000 to $10,000 each. In addition, no check signed by President Ford has ever been offered on the open market.

The rarest signed White House cards are those of Presidents Garfield, Grant, and Benjamin Harrison. The hardest-to-get signed photographs are those of Presidents Buchanan, Fillmore, Pierce, Tyler, and Van Buren.

Presidents William Henry Harrison and James A. Garfield offer the most difficult challenge to collectors. Harrison served just one month, and Garfield only four. While papers signed prior to their terms in office are more readily available, there are few documents signed during their short terms as president.

Don't expect to find presidential autographs hidden away in an attic trunk. Most dealers agree that 95 percent of all presidential autographs have been discovered; they are either in the collections of private owners or are available for sale via dealers and auction houses. This means you have to rely on the latter for the signatures you want.

Where to Buy Your Autographs

When you purchase autographs, it is important to buy from a source you trust implicitly, one that will *guarantee* the autograph to be genuine. I can't stress this enough. If you wind up with something phony, you'll have a difficult time getting your money back without such a guarantee.

Here are some leading autograph auction houses. All, to our knowledge, offer certificates of authenticity with every autograph they sell.

Charles Hamilton Galleries, Inc.
25 East 77th Street
New York, NY 10021

Phillips
867 Madison Avenue
New York, NY 10022

Daniel F. Kelleher Co., Inc.
Ten Post Office Square #1230
Boston, MA 02109

Sotheby, Parke Bernet
1334 York Avenue
New York, NY 10021

Swann Galleries
104 East 25th Street
New York, NY 10010

Here are the names of other major dealers in the country:

Abraham Lincoln Book Shop
18 East Chestnut Street
Chicago, IL 60611

American Collectibles
P.O. Box 57
Lewiston, NY 14092

Autograph Alcove
1104 N. Third Street
Milwaukee, WI 53203

Robert F. Batchelder
One West Butler Avenue
Ambler, PA 19002

Walter R. Benjamin, Autographs
790 Madison Avenue
New York, NY 10021

Carnegie Book Shop
140 East 59th Street
New York, NY 10022

Conway Barker
P. O. Box 30625
Dallas, TX 75230

Herman M. Darvick
P.O. Box 467
Rockville Centre, NY 11571

Raleigh DeGeer Amyx
21303 Sheriff Court
Vienna, VA 22180

Federal Hill Autographs
P.O. Box 6405
Baltimore, MD 21230

Goodspeed's Book Shop
18 Beacon Street
Boston, MA 02108

Doris Harris, Autographs
6381 Hollywood Boulevard
Los Angeles, CA 90028

John Howell, Books
434 Post Street
San Francisco, CA 94102

J.F.F. Autographs
P.O. Box U
Manhasset, NY 11030

Robert Kuhn Autographs
720 Geary Street
San Francisco, CA 94101

Lion Heart Autograph, Inc.
12 W. 37th Street #1212
New York, NY 10018

Lone Star Autographs
P.O. Box 668
Forney, TX 75126

James Lowe, Autographs
667 Madison Avenue
New York, NY 10021

Monetary Investment, Ltd.
P.O. Box 17246
Milwaukee, WI 53217

Julia Sweet Newman
P.O. Box 156
Battle Creek, MI 49016

Kenneth W. Rendell, Inc.
154 Wells Avenue
Newton, MA 02159

Paul C. Richards
High Acres
Templeton, MA 01468

Joseph Rubinfine
R.F.D. #1
Pleasantville, NJ 08232

Rosejeanne Slifer
30 Park Avenue
New York, NY 10016

This list is by no means complete. We suggest you contact
other dealers through your local phone book, collector's magazines, and other sources.

No matter where you purchase autographs, make sure you get a firm, money-back guarantee *in writing*—plus a certificate of authenticity. These are your best protection against fraud.

What Should I Buy?

There are two ways to collect autographs, according to Robert Batchelder, a noted dealer in the Philadelphia area. The first is to acquire the very best you can from dealers and auction houses. The second is to write letters to famous people. When using the second approach, don't just ask for their autograph. Request the reason for their success—or their happiest moment. Give them something to respond to.

Philip Sang, a prominent Illinois businessman who passed away a few years ago, was amazingly successful at the first method of collecting. He began collecting autographs in the 1950s and amassed a collection that included many colonial figures, Revolutionary War heroes, and signers of the Declaration of Independence and the Constitution. He also owned some important letters written by Abraham Lincoln and George Washington. Since his death, his collection has brought several million dollars in five different auctions.

Batchelder says that many items in Sang's collection sold for ten times what he paid for them. "Collections of this kind," he adds, "should show the same kind of growth in the next 20 years as they have in the past 20."

Using the second method is also profitable. Many famous collections, says Batchelder, got their start when the collector wrote letters to famous people. "Collections like these usually do not have a high value per item, though, because contemporary people have written thousands of letters and answered many requests for autographs."

For this second method, a novel approach is necessary to evoke a good response. Also, if you wish to collect presidential autographs, it's best to catch people *before* they become president. Try to anticipate possible winners and write to them before they're elected. This will not only go a long way toward assuring that you get a reply, it will also prevent your receiving a robot signature.

What Is
a Robot Signature?

A robot signature is, as its name implies, one made by a machine. Such a practice has become commonplace among modern presidents—and the signatures are virtually worthless. As a matter of fact, many are considered fakes.

How to Preserve
Your Autographs and Documents

There are a variety of reasons why paper deteriorates: careless handling, pollution, insects, sunlight, heat, humidity, and chemicals in contact with or within the paper itself. You can do several things, however, to protect valuable documents and autographs:

1. Keep them in a cool, dry place. Avoid hanging them over fireplaces, heat vents, radiators, or in bathrooms.

2. Keep them out of direct sunlight or high-intensity lights. Any inked document can fade.

3. Your documents need to breathe. That's why it's wise to keep them in acid-free folders that protect them and allow

them to adjust naturally to their environment. Acid-free folders can be obtained from University Products, Box 101, Holyoke, MA 01041.

4. When handling your documents, be sure your hands are free of oil, grease, and dirt. Support the document firmly; don't hold it by one corner, but don't be afraid of it; handle it carefully but with authority. Do not smoke, eat, or drink while handling it. And be especially careful of minute tears around the perimeter; these easily become big tears.

5. If you want to frame your documents, be sure you deal with a professional conservation framer, who will use neutral pH or buffered archival-quality matboard. All hanging material should be acid free.

6. Never use pressure-sensitive tape on or near your documents. And never, under any circumstances, use cellophane tape for repairs; it will eventually yellow and stain your document.

The proper preservation of your documents will help maintain and increase their value in future years—as well as add to your personal enjoyment.

Publications
You Should Read

Pen and Quill, published by the Universal Autograph Collector's Club, is a great help to beginners. The $12 membership fee gets you the magazine and puts you on the mailing lists of autograph dealers, which is the best way to discover what's available. Write: P. O. Box 467 Rockville Centre, NY 11571.

Manuscripts, published by the Manuscript Society, is a more sophisticated publication and is available for a $20 membership fee. Write: 350 North Niagara Street, Burbank, CA 91505.

If you want to see the publication before subscribing, ask for a sample copy of the most recent issue.

How to Profit From Presidential Autographs

While there are a variety of ways to profit from presidential letters and autographs, this should not be your only reason for collecting them. Enjoy what you have for its historical and educational value, then explore one of the following potential avenues of resale.

Sell to Other Collectors

Thousands of people are fascinated by American history and would love to own a piece of it. Many people, however, don't realize these valuable autographs are available for sale. You can reach these people through classified ads in collectors' publications and in local newspapers. Advertise one specific autograph or entice customers with a general ad. A general ad will probably lead to more inquiries and could even help you start your own business, which we'll talk about in a subsequent chapter.

Here are several publications ripe for such advertisements. Their readers know the advantages of collecting presidential autographs and you shouldn't have much competition from other sellers. In addition, their classified ad rates are very low.

American Collectibles, Inc.
P.O. Box 57
Lewiston, NY 14092

Antique and Collector's Mart
15100 West Kellogg
Wichita, KS 67235

Linn's Stamp News
P. O. Box 29
Sidney, OH 45367

Members of the Universal Autograph Collector's Club are entitled to place a free classified advertisement in the club's publication, *The Pen & Quill*. This is a fine way to meet other collectors and to build a customer list.

Remember not to ignore local newspapers. Potential customers may be right around the corner.

Sell to Historical Institutions and Museums

In spite of economic hardships, many of our country's museums are still pursuing the collection of letters and documents to expand their archives. Most large-city historical societies employ full-time staffs to seek such items. University libraries have grants and other funds to purchase documents and letters, and even the earliest presidents have historical libraries containing their papers. These libraries are usually located in the president's birthplace, home town, or university.

If you donate your collection (or part of it) to one of these institutions you may gain some tax advantages. Consult an accountant before making any donation for tax purposes, however, to make sure it will benefit you.

Sell Through Auctions

These historical treasures have been bringing higher and higher prices at auction. Auctions are where the "real" collectors go; people who are looking for a specific document and are willing to spend the money to get it.

Contact the auction houses mentioned earlier in this chapter and others. Determine when the next sale is and how many documents will be auctioned. (Some houses wait until they have a large number, then auction all off at once.) Find out what the seller's fee is (usually 10 to 25 percent) and use that to establish an acceptable minimum bid.

Sell to Retail Stores

This is a truly imaginative avenue for the prospective seller. There might be a restaurant, bar, or a fine retail furniture or gift store in your area that has an historical or presidential motif. Many of these stores like to display (and sometimes sell) these items. A number of major department stores (such as Altman's in New York City) also sell presidential autographs. Use your instincts and imagination and you may find a whole new line of potential buyers. Of course, don't forget conventional autograph dealers, who are usually on the lookout for autographs requested by their customers.

No matter how you sell your presidential autographs, your certificate of authenticity is the key. You can assure buyers your document is indeed authentic by giving them the certificate and document to examine, which they can take to a third party, and by offering a money-back guarantee.

The Value of Presidential Autographs

The value of a particular presidential autograph depends on a number of factors—its rarity, its context (personal letter or presidential document), and the popularity of that president. Here are some presidential autographs recently put up for sale by a major New York dealer:

President	Dated	Price
U. S. Grant	Dec. 21, 1874	$225.00
Harry Truman	Dec. 9, 1957	235.00
Zachary Taylor	Dec. 1, 1835	495.00

Warren Harding	Sept. 21, 1921	595.00
Benjamin Harrison	March 16, 1892	350.00
James Monroe/	June 30, 1824	1,250.00
Abraham Lincoln	July 19, 1862	2,250.00
George Washington	June, 1783	3,000.00
Thomas Jefferson	Oct. 10, 1793	4,750.00

You can get a sample of the latest offerings in this field and current prices, at no charge, by writing American Collectibles, P.O. Box 57, Lewiston, NY 14092.

7

Choosing Tomorrow's Collectible Winners Today

In 1962 noted stamp collector H. E. Harris went to court to prevent the postal authorities of the Panama Canal Zone from reprinting an error stamp. The reprinting would have destroyed the value of Harris' discovery, and a number of courts ruled that the government could not interfere with Harris' find. Today, this rare stamp is worth more than $10,000.

In 1966, the Beatles issued a record album with an extremely controversial cover. The album was pulled out of the stores almost immediately after its release. It was subsequently reissued with a different cover. Today that album, "Yesterday and Today," is worth $8 to $10 with the second cover. With the original controversial cover? $600!

These examples point out the central factor that makes a collectible valuable—rarity. If collecting baseball cards for resale had been in vogue 30 or 40 years ago, many of today's high-priced cards would be virtually worthless, for there would be a glut of them on the market. But many of our mothers threw away these childhood toys that are now worth, in some cases, thousands of dollars. You hear stories like these from people all the time—of virtual treasure chests stored in attics and later thrown out.

The first *Superman* comic book; the 1952 Mickey Mantle baseball card; an Elvis Presley record on the Sun label. Who knew 20, 30, or 40 years ago that there would be a market for these items in the 1980s? The people who got rid of items like these helped create the collectibles boom that other people are enjoying today.

In early 1981, as we've mentioned, Alan Shawn Feinstein recommended a list of 53 error stamps to the readers of his private newsletter. Alan concluded these stamps were ready for a big move. They were rare, they had unique appeal, and they were grossly undervalued. In the six months after his recommendation, the value of these stamps increased more than gold, silver, diamonds, stocks, or bonds. In fact, *every one* of Alan Shawn Feinstein's readers who got these stamps in early 1981 on his recommendation was offered a substantial profit on them. And these stamps should continue to go up in value, he says, year after year.

Alan says the same thing about U.S. presidential autographs. They are rare—only 39 men have held the office. They have value as historical documents. There is growing demand for them—as evidenced by the prices paid for presidential documents. They are grossly undervalued, considering their rarity. All these factors lead to the conclusion that they have exceptional appreciation potential.

Almost any collectible you can think of can be put to the same test. Let's examine the ways in which you can find out the potential value of such collectibles.

What Determines Value?

The Item Has
Intrinsic Value

In an earlier chapter, you read of Alan's amazing success with silver a few years ago. When Alan made his purchase, he bought silver coin futures rather than pure silver futures. Why?

Because the coins would never be worth less than their face value. It lessened the risk Alan was taking.

The Item Has
a Limited Supply

Remember that much of a collectible's worth is based on the simple economic rule of supply and demand. If supply is limited and demand intense, the price is high. If supply is abundant and demand minimal, the price is low. This is true not only for collectibles, but for everyday items such as calculators and cars, shoes and stereos, airfares and avocados.

Error stamps and presidential autographs are typical examples of this rule; only a very small number are available. This leaves collectors with very few to choose from, resulting in growing demand and an ever-shrinking available supply.

Demonetized bank notes also fall into this category. No more will ever be printed. Demand for them may rise, but the supply will never increase. That is one reason why Alan feels they will be increasingly valuable in years to come.

There Is Already
a Demand for the Item

Even if there is only a small demand for an item, it may have potential growth appeal. Demand can, and many times does, spread because people hear about a particular collectible and then want to purchase it themselves.

This is what happened with baseball cards. Ten or 15 years ago, there were relatively few baseball card collectors. Then word got around that baseball cards were bringing high prices. People started attending collector's shows, bringing a haul from their attics. Soon, dealers began opening stores devoted entirely to baseball cards and other sports collectibles. While demand was increasing, the available supply was decreasing. It is one reason why many baseball cards have risen in value so much in recent years.

There Is
Potential Growth Appeal

When a low supply and a high demand serve to drive up an item's price, its long-term profitability can be hurt. Once the price reaches a certain level, it may stagnate for quite a while and collectors buying it at the high price may have to wait some time before they can sell it at a good profit.

This is one reason that Alan Shawn Feinstein urges people to be cautious in bidding for anything. Bidding wars can drive prices above an item's value, severely dampening its future appreciation potential. That is why Alan suggests never bidding higher than 10 to 15 percent over the last auction price.

Recent excessive price jumps are one reason why, at present, baseball cards are not a good opportunity for people just getting started. The prices are already prohibitive, and the prices for many rare cards have already hit extremely high levels.

If you can get in on the ground floor, the growth appeal can be phenomenal. If you come in in the middle, that growth appeal is less. If you try to enter at the top, you may find it's already too late.

The Item Is
Grossly Undervalued

This may be the most difficult part of the test to measure. Every individual has a different idea about the value of a collectible. One thing is for certain, though. If you can get something for not much more than its face value, its downside risk is limited while its profit potential can be tremendous.

"Buy, if you can, when other people think it's practically worthless," says Alan Shawn Feinstein. "That is when you can get it at *real* low prices—with limited risk at those prices and unlimited potential."

Of the five parts to this test, supply and demand are probably the most important. If the supply is static or shrinking, the potential for growing value is strong. Even if there is little or no present demand, it can develop slowly. Buy the collectibles you like, ones in shrinking supply, and hold on to them until a growing demand and active marketplace arise for them. Then watch their value climb.

How Does a Market Develop?

Some factors that can lead to the growth of a market for a particular collectible are simply related to outside influences.

1. *Media.* The news media can have a dramatic impact on the market value of a collectible. A newspaper article about rare autographs, for example, can increase the desire of some people to own them. The success of baseball cards is due in part to the publicity they received early on. A camera crew would film a story about a local card show. Soon people were checking their basements and trunks. A new dimension was added to something that was once just a hobby.

Stay informed about collectibles. You may find an article about a collector who is looking for an item you possess. The news media can reach many people. It is a powerful force in today's collectibles market.

2. *Mania.* Events that we have no control over can sometimes create a collectible market by themselves. Elvis Presley's death sent people scurrying for old records and memorabilia. The murder of John Lennon had the same impact. Suddenly, Beatles memorabilia was selling for record prices. When an item

is attached to a significant event, it often finds its own market. People will attach value to an item related to an important happening.

3. *People*. People can create a market on their own. If someone is willing to spend a large amount of money for an item, a whole new market can be created. Remember, you can sell anything if there is someone out there willing to buy it.

Looking to the Future

How can you tell if something you now possess might be valuable in years to come? One way is to judge what items have become popular collectibles in the last few years. Many are connected with nostalgia—baseball cards, old comic books, and rare phonograph records remind people of days gone by. The many fond memories connected to these things is certainly one reason for their popularity.

Rarity—limited supply—plays a large part in determining the future value of a collectible. It is one factor we constantly stress because of its importance.

Today, demand is growing for items like antique toys, rare postcards, old phonograph records, and similar collectibles. If you have things like these stored away, it is certainly worth your time to check into their value. A book called *The Encyclopedia of Associations*, which you can get at the library, lists dozens of clubs for all types of collectors. Many of these groups have their own publications or can tell you about other ones.

Is It Time to Sell?

If you can afford to keep a collectible for a few years, it is always wise to do so. Chances are you won't get less than the present value. Good collectibles generally tend to grow in value over the years. And of course there is always the possibility that the price will rise dramatically.

If and when you do sell, remember to check all avenues—dealers, collectors' publications, advertisements in local newspapers, and possibly auctions. Search carefully to be sure you end up selling at the best price you can.

What About Buying?

No matter what kind of collectible you want, always get it for the lowest possible price. You may find some collectibles at flea markets, others at auction or expensive antique stores. Don't buy until you are absolutely sure you cannot acquire the item for a lower price.

In Conclusion

If it were easy to predict where the next collectible boom was coming from there would be many wealthy collectors. How many times have you kicked yourself because you've thrown out baseball cards, comic books, or autograph collections?

Use Alan Shawn Feinstein's guidelines as much as possible. They can help you make important decisions about buying and selling, and substantially increase your profit potential.

Don't forget what determines growth appeal:

- A limited supply
- A growing demand
- Buying at the lowest prices you can find

It's a formula that may help you turn today's junk into tomorrow's treasure.

8

How to Avoid Counterfeit Collectibles

How would you feel if you spent $1,500 on an autographed Abraham Lincoln letter only to find out later that it was a counterfeit? The faking of collectibles is something you must be aware of. With items such as stamps, gems, and autographs bringing higher and higher prices, the door is open to unscrupulous people who seek to defraud the public.

Fortunately there are things you can do to ensure you are getting authentic collectibles; ways you can make sure your money is well spent.

The old expression "you get what you pay for" is one of the most important things you will get out of this chapter. When purchasing any collectible, keep in mind that everyone is looking for a bargain, especially in these times of tight money and high prices. With collectibles, though, something that's too good to be true, priced *far* below its worth, probably is a fake.

This is not to say that everything with a low (or relatively low) price tag is ersatz. There may be occasions when a collectible, for one reason or another, is selling for a ridiculously low price. Perhaps the seller has a cash-flow problem or wants money for something else—or is selling the collectible as a loss leader to attract business for other items. You may get lucky and find a seller in such a position. In such a case, you're able to buy what you're looking for at a very lost price. These occasions, however, are few and far between.

Hustlers, like muggers, can spot a potential victim a mile away. Someone who is eager to buy and anxious to make a quick buck is a perfect target for a counterfeiter. Counterfeiters know what spurs their victims on. On a smaller scale, it's almost like buying a $300 watch on the street for $25 and seeing it break in three days.

It takes a realistic attitude to deal in collectibles. While you may find something for a relatively low price, chances of getting a real bargain are slim. If you know the market and are aware of current price trends, you should be able to spot a potential fake rather easily. Remember, if the price seems too good to be true, it usually is.

Avoiding the Counterfeiters

The surest way to avoid being taken by a counterfeiter is to buy only from reputable dealers and auction houses that will provide you with guarantees and certificates of authenticity. We discuss choosing a dealer in greater detail in a subsequent chapter, but the basic rule is this: Find reputable dealers through collectors you already know or through companies listed in this book.

Now let's point out some of the ways you can protect yourself from counterfeits and forgeries—in each of Alan's four recommended categories.

Error Stamps

Although error stamps might seem ripe for counterfeiting, you have a distinct protection against this type of fraud. As mentioned previously, most error stamps are currently handled only by auction houses that specialize in them. These auctioneers are very knowledgeable and careful about what they accept, and you can be sure you're not getting counterfeit stamps when you deal with reputable auction houses.

Then, too, counterfeiting error stamps is not easy. Chemical processes used to remove particular colors do not always work, particularly if two or more colors are blended together. It is almost impossible to get all of one color out of a stamp. This type of tampering usually leaves specks of color, making the stamp merely a freak instead of an error.

A fairly new counterfeiting technique involves the use of lasers to remove color. This practice is not easy to detect, but fortunately it is also not widespread.

To ensure your peace of mind when you purchase an error stamp, contact the American Philatelic Society (which has ties to the U.S. mint) on anything you buy unless it is guaranteed by a well-known dealer. The APS will evaluate any error stamp for you, if you wish, and contact the mint to determine if and how such an error occurred. Their fee is $3 to $5 per stamp, and their address is P.O. Box 800, State College, PA 16801.

Incidentally, most reputable auction houses do their own legwork when they acquire an error stamp. They contact the mint for the same kind of information the American Philatelic Society does. If you want to be absolutely sure your stamp is genuine, though, the Society will be happy to perform this service.

Most auction houses will also guarantee the authenticity of the stamps they sell. If they will not, do not purchase from them.

If you find a dealer who sells error stamps (or other rare stamps), always purchase them on approval or with a guarantee. You can usually get a 30-day money-back guarantee. If not, don't buy.

Use the guarantee period to get second and third opinions about the stamps. You can take them to other dealers or to friends who collect stamps. If, after talking to other people, you have any doubts, return the stamps to the dealer and get your money back.

Make sure the dealer writes the exact condition of the stamp on the invoice. If he claims it to be in mint, never-hinged condition, that is what your receipt should say. It is the best protection you have against fraud.

Demonetized Bank Notes

Counterfeiters have not gotten involved in common inexpensive bank notes—yet. At the present time, prices are too low to interest forgers. But if prices increase as expected, you can bet the counterfeiters won't be more than a step behind.

As with other collectibles, make sure you're buying from a reputable dealer. Get a money-back guarantee and seek second and third opinions.

Gemstones

At present, certification of colored gemstones is a new procedure. There are no exact standards for certification and much of the work is done by eye. Thus, it is a very subjective determination. Emeralds, rubies, or sapphires guaranteed to be of certain specifications by one gemologist may get a different grading from another.

Again, when searching for a dealer or wholesaler of colored gems, find someone you can trust. Get a strong guarantee, and if possible a certificate of authenticity. As we said, certification for grading purposes is a problem; certificates of authenticity, however, should not be.

Alan also recommends that you stay away from gemstones offered for a fraction of their value. Although these may not be counterfeit gems, they are probably man-made. Anything that can be manufactured will have an unlimited supply, thus, the value of such synthetic stones has little or no growth potential.

Presidential Autographs

The biggest problems with presidential signatures and documents is not counterfeiting, but the use of "autopens" or "robot pens"—machines that can reproduce a signature with an incredible degree of accuracy.

Lee Simonson (American Collectibles, Lewiston, New York) says, "Many of our modern presidents used auto pens. John F. Kennedy used them all the time. Even though it's hard to differentiate machine-made signatures from the real thing, they are fakes and are worthless."

The key, according to Simonson, is the usual one: to deal only with a reputable dealer or auction house. Most offer an unconditional guarantee with this provision: If two leading experts concur that the signature is a fake, you can get your money back—up to ten years later.

"Independent handwriting analysts are a waste of time," Simonson adds. "Your best protection is to deal with the people who deal with the product."

Every reputable autograph dealer and auction house knows the source and genuineness of any signatures purchased. Your best protection then, as Simonson said, is to find a dealer or auction house you can trust. If a friend or acquaintance collects autographs, find out who his dealer is. And, of course, never purchase an autograph without a money-back guarantee and a certificate of authenticity.

Getting Second Opinions

If you were thinking of buying a car, you would go to more than one dealer. If a doctor recommended surgery, you would generally see a specialist for another opinion. Yet many people who buy collectibles fail to get a second opinion.

Even if you implicitly trust the seller from whom you are buying, the importance of another opinion can't be stressed often enough. Even a dealer can make a mistake—and if you don't catch it, you'll get an unwelcome surprise when you decide to sell.

There are various places to obtain second and third opinions. Other dealers in your area should be willing to examine an item you bought from someone else. If you have a friend with more experience in the field than you, he can probably direct you to someone. And many collectors' publications contain advertisements from people who will examine stamps, autographs, and the like. They will usually charge for their services, but if you did not buy your collectible from an established, trusted source, it is worth it—if only for your own peace of mind.

Purchasing on Approval

Purchasing on approval is similar to a money-back guarantee, except that you don't have to pay for the item until you examine it.

This is common for mail-order firms that deal in stamps. You order something to purchase on approval. You are given a certain period of time to examine it, after which time you can purchase it or return it and owe nothing.

If you order anything through the mails from a firm you do not know, you should purchase *only* on approval. This is not to say that a firm that does not allow you to purchase on approval is disreputable. It is, however, the only way we recommend you buy from a stranger.

Money-back Guarantees

Money-back guarantees are your best protection when buying from anyone. The stronger the guarantee, the better off you are. Always attempt to get a 30-day, money-back guarantee.

Also, remember to get the condition of the item in writing, preferably on the invoice. It will help you to avoid a futile confrontation if you later discover the item isn't what the dealer said it was. Remember that your position with a dealer is only as strong as the guarantee you receive. Any dealer who refuses to give you a guarantee should be avoided.

Certificates of Authenticity

Certificates of authenticity are common to gems, presidential autographs, and other high-priced collectibles. They act not only as guarantees, but they serve as a measure of protection if you attempt to sell the items.

Most reputable auction houses and many dealers offer certificates of authenticity with everything they sell. It is your best protection because it is in writing. Always retain these certificates. You will need them if you ever decide to sell.

In Conclusion

People who are defrauded often allow themselves to be Whether it's due to carelessness, an attempt to get something for nothing, or sheer ignorance about counterfeiting, many people needlessly become victims.

You can protect yourself! Guarantees, approval purchases, and certificates of authenticity are available to help you avoid being defrauded. Second, third, and even fourth opinions are readily available—if you take the time and make the effort to seek them out. Remember that many counterfeits and forgeries are so good only an expert can spot them. That is why we stress over and over again the importance of buying only from reputable dealers and auction houses.

9

What You Should Know About Dealers and Auction Houses

Stan Smith (not his real name) was just getting started in stamp collecting a few years ago. He didn't know any dealers, so he chose one at random out of the phone book. Stan told the dealer about the types of stamps and the kind of profits he was looking for. The dealer sold him a few issues for which Stan paid $385. Assured that each stamp was in mint condition and had never been hinged, Stan took the stamps home, excited about his new venture.

A few months later, Stan was showing his growing collection to a business acquaintance who had had some experience with stamps. Stan boasted about the incredibly low prices he paid for stamps in mint condition. His experienced friend examined the stamps and gave Stan some very discouraging news. The stamps, in fact, had been regummed, and they were *not* in mint condition; the margins of one stamp were not uniform, and another was slightly soiled.

Stan discovered that the stamps he had would not appreciate in value as much as if they had been in the mint condition the dealer had claimed they were. Furious, he complained to the dealer, who denied ever claiming the stamps were in mint condition. Stan's invoice made no mention of the stamps' condition. Stan was out of luck—and out of a good chunk of his original investment.

Choosing a Dealer

People recommend doctors, lawyers, and merchants every day of the year. You should attempt to use the same approach when you search for a dealer of collectibles.

The best way to find a dealer is through someone you know. A personal recommendation from someone you trust is the best assurance you can have of a dealer's integrity. You probably know a handful of people who collect stamps, coins, or other items. Even if you don't, your friends probably know someone who does.

If you cannot find a dealer through a recommendation, there are some other routes you can take. Each has its pitfalls, however, so you must use extreme caution.

Your local phone book probably lists a large number of dealers for whatever type of collectible that interests you. You should call as many dealers as necessary until you find one with whom you feel comfortable. There are a number of questions that every dealer should be able to answer.

Your local newspaper may contain classified or display advertisements placed by local dealers. In many Sunday newspapers, a "leisure" section contains dozens of such ads.

Collectors' clubs can also be a source of valuable assistance. It may take some digging to find one of these clubs, but the people in these clubs probably have the experience you lack. They often place notices of their meetings in special-interest magazines and local newspapers. Collectors' publications also usually contain ads from dealers across the country, but you can't automatically assume that the dealers that advertise in these publications are reputable, so be careful.

If you choose a local dealer, you may want to check his reputation. Your state probably has a consumer protection agency located within the state attorney general's office. A county agency would probably be a part of the prosecutor's office. These agencies should be able to tell you whether the dealer in question has had any complaints lodged against him by consumers.

The Facts You
Should Tell Every Dealer

Dealers of collectibles, like clothing stores and department stores, are in business to make money. They are also in business to please their customers.

With any dealer, you should be as forthcoming as you can. Explain your specific interest—if stamps, which type of stamps you want; if gems, the size and type you want; if autographs, the types of signatures you are most interested in acquiring. If the dealer knows what you're looking for, he can better help you get it.

Don't hesitate to inform a dealer that you are looking for resale potential. It will indicate to him that you will be a valuable customer if he meets your needs. It will also tell him that you are prepared to spend money if an item is potentially valuable.

Tell him that you want to acquire these items for the lowest possible price, but make him understand that you are in for the long term. A smart dealer will sacrifice a few dollars for your future business.

Following are some things you should attempt to find out from any dealer you contact.

1. Ask for a certificate of authenticity or a written statement describing the condition of any item you buy. In many cases, such a certificate will be necessary to resell a collectible easily. A written statement of condition is important if you discover the item is not in the condition the dealer said it was in. If you attempt to get a refund, this will help you.

2. Make sure you understand the dealer's refund policy. Most coin dealers offer at least a seven-day return privilege for unsatisfactory material, a practice dealers of other collectibles should adopt. Alan Shawn Feinstein strongly recommends that you get a 30-day, money-back guarantee signed by the dealer, and that the guarantee be for a cash refund, not for a

credit towards other purchases. Your guarantee is a strong measure of protection; make sure the dealer offers a fair one.

3. Ask the dealer to give you the names and phone numbers of a few of his customers. You can contact these people and ask their opinion of the dealer. A reputable dealer with satisfied customers should have no problem complying with such a request.

4. Ask the dealer if he will try to obtain other items that you desire if he doesn't have them in stock. A dealer who is willing to do this for you wants your business. You'll both benefit.

Buying from Local Dealers

After finding a dealer you trust, there are some steps you should take when deciding whether to purchase anything.

1. Once a dealer quotes you a price, check it with some other dealers. (That's why it is advantageous to find more than one dealer with whom you can do business.) Remember, always get the lowest possible price. Your attempts to haggle on price may or may not be successful, depending on the dealer.

2. Don't settle for anyting other than exactly what you want. If you have any reason to suspect that the condition of the item is not what it seems to be, *don't buy it*. There will be other opportunities. If the dealer doesn't have the item you want, don't let him steer you toward anything else. You must acquire patience when dealing in collectibles—the patience to wait for the right opportunity, and the patience to let your purchases appreciate in value.

3. Before your guarantee runs out, take the item to another dealer for a second opinion. You should be 100 percent sure about the quality, condition, price, and potential resale value before you decide to keep the item. If you—or other people

whom you show it to—disagree with the dealer's opinion, you might be better off getting a refund and waiting for another opportunity.

Buying Through the Mails

This is a common practice for purchasing stamps, coins, and autographs. When you buy through the mail, however, you buy sight unseen.

That is why we strongly recommend that when you buy through the mail, you buy only on approval, *or* with a return privilege. If you purchase collectibles by mail, it is the only protection you have.

When you purchase on approval, you have the right to examine the items at no charge. If they are to your liking, you pay for them. If not, simply return them—promptly.

But when you buy this way, always get second and third opinions. You may find a dealer who can get you the same item for a lower price.

Buying Through Auctions

If you are interested in extremely rare and expensive collectibles, auction houses are probably your best bet. Sellers find them advantageous because they can dispose of their collectibles without too much effort.

There are many reputable auction houses throughout the country for all types of collectibles. (In each of the chapters about specific collectibles, you will find a list of auction houses.)

When you buy at auction, you are usually guaranteed authenticity and quality. Competitive bidding, however, makes it difficult to get the lowest possible price. This depends entirely on whether the auction is attended mainly by collectors or by dealers. Coin and gem auctions are attended mostly by the latter, so a collector bidding against them can get material at wholesale—an incredible savings. I've saved at least $2,500 by bidding at public auctions.

If you decide to purchase at auction, there are a few things you should find out before placing a bid.

1. Obtain a catalogue from the auction house. It will explain in detail the times that auctions will be held and the minimum (or reserve) bid, if any. If you live near the area where the auction will be held, it makes sense to examine the items in person.

2. If possible, obtain a list of the latest prices realized for the same or similar items. It will give you an idea of the prices you can expect to pay. Remember, though, that competitive bidding offers no guarantees. If some collector who desperately wants a particular collectible attends the auction, the bids can be driven up significantly.

Again, we warn you against becoming involved in a bidding war. Never pay more than 10 to 15 percent over the most recent auction price for the item you want. You may lose it to another bidder, but you will have other opportunities. Dramatic price increases from one auction to the next only serve to diminish the *future* growth potential of the item in question.

3. Find out what type of a buyer's commission the auction house collects (it can run anywhere from 10 to 25 percent of the resale price). If, for example, you buy a rare autograph for $1,000 and the buyer's fee is 25 percent, you'll actually pay $1,250. Remember this whenever you buy at auction.

4. Don't lock yourself out of an auction because it is not being held in your area. Ask the auction house if you can bid by mail, or send someone else to bid for you. The former depends on the auction house, the latter should always be acceptable.

If you do bid by mail, you are often bidding blindly. There is no way you can tell what the competition will be for the item that you want, and you do not have the advantage of upping your bid once the auction starts.

If you cannot attend the auction, it is better to send someone to do your bidding for you. Perhaps you have a friend or relative who can attend; dealers attending an auction will usually execute your bids for a 5 percent commission. Just make sure that your representative knows the maximum amount you are prepared to spend.

Selling Your Collectibles

There will come a time, two to five years from now, when you want to sell some of the collectibles you have acquired. There are a variety of ways to sell what you own, some more advantageous than others.

Selling Through Dealers

This is probably the *least* advantageous way to sell your collectibles. It is an avenue that may be considered, but unless you're extremely lucky, you will find better ways to sell. Dealers, as we've said, are in business to make money. Price markups are as common to dealers of collectibles as they are to other types of merchants.

Assume, for example, that you own a rare stamp worth $3,000. If a dealer accepts your price, he must raise the asking price to the next buyer in order to make a profit. If the dealer doesn't think he can sell at a profit, he probably won't buy or may try to get you to lower your asking price. Don't! You can probably do better elsewhere.

The only time you may get your price from a dealer is if he has a customer who wants exactly what you have. The odds of that, of course, are slim. However, you may find a dealer who is willing to sell on consignment. The dealer takes the item after you've established the price you want for it. If the dealer sells, you receive your money.

Be aware of this, however: If you place an item on consignment, you take it off the marketplace. You may miss an opportunity to sell it elsewhere. Guard against this possibility by getting a written agreement with the dealer, establishing a time frame for selling the item as well as the price you are to receive.

The dealer may want a commission or may mark up the item to give himself a profit. Whatever the case, make sure you have a signed agreement.

Selling Through Auctions

Selling your collectibles at auction can be very fruitful, but there are some pitfalls to be aware of. Auctions are good for sellers because collectors who buy at auction know what they want and are prepared to spend the money necessary to obtain it. Your involvement is minimal and the chances of getting your asking price (or more) are good.

If you choose to sell at auction, there are a number of things you should check before you turn over your items:

1. Obtain a copy of the latest realized auction prices for items you want to sell. You will get an idea of what you can expect to make and you may decide it isn't the time to sell.

2. Sellers as well as buyers pay a commission to the auction house. The seller's fee is normally the same as the buyer's fee, and can vary anywhere from 10 to 25 percent. This fee will play a part in how much you ask for your items.

3. Establish a reserve, or minimum acceptable bid, with the auction house. When you set this bid, don't forget to figure in the commission. Let's take the $3,000 stamp, for example. If that stamp is auctioned for $3,000 and the house commission is 25 percent, you will receive only $2,250. To realize $3,000,

your stamp must sell for $4,000! It is an important point to remember, and is one of the problems connected with selling at auction.

4. Determine what other items will be up for sale at that auction. If there are too many error stamps, for example, they will compete with one another and you may lose your selling leverage. There may be other error stamps with smaller minimum bids that make them more attractive than yours.

Selling at auction is largely a guessing game. There is no sure way to tell whether you will get the price you want. The commissions the auction house receives can be a prohibitive factor to both buyers and sellers. Remember though that an auction house can probably find more prospective buyers than a dealer can.

Selling Directly
to Other Collectors

This is a method of selling that can be very profitable for both buyer and seller. It does require more involvement on your part, since you must place ads and talk to prospective buyers.

Selling directly to another collector effectively cuts out the middleman, whether it be an auction house or a dealer. You don't have to increase your asking price to cover the house commission, and the buyer doesn't have to figure it into his expenses.

If this is the route you choose (and it is one that should be explored), place ads in collectors' publications and local newspapers. Be very specific about what you are selling, although it isn't necessary to mention the price you want. "Best offer above $_____ accepted" is enough to get you some serious bids and scare off people who can't afford your price.

If you are successful, do not accept anything other than a certified check or money order as payment. If the buyer is local and offers you a personal check, make sure it clears the bank before you turn over the item.

If you have the time and effort to sell on your own, that is the way you should go. You are more likely to get the price you want when neither party has to worry about commissions and dealer markups.

How to Profit
from This Chapter

1. Shop for a dealer the way you would for any other consumer item. Ask important questions and make sure the answers satisfy you. Find out about the refund policy and the dealer's reputation.

2. Don't limit yourself to a small number of dealers. The more you speak with, the greater your chances of finding one whom you trust.

3. Investigate the possibility of buying and selling directly with other collectors. Both parties can save on commissions and dealer markups.

4. Accept no less than a 30-day, money-back guarantee from anyone. Investigate the possibility of getting an unconditional money-back guarantee; some dealers now offer this.

5. Make sure you obtain in writing the condition, description, and price of anything you buy. This protection is essential.

6. If you sell at auction, determine how many similar items will also be on sale. If there are more than one or two, wait for the next auction. You want all the selling power you can get.

10

Starting Your Own Part-Time Business in Collectibles

Many people find unique opportunities to start their own part-time businesses in collectibles. Diane Ray (not her real name) of Wichita Falls, Texas, came up with one such idea.

Diane acquired a few bank notes and thought they would look lovely framed. She read some books about conservation framing, purchased the necessary materials, and framed the few she owned.

Then she realized there were people who had autographs, bank notes, and other documents they might want preserved. Diane took out a few small classified ads advertising her service in local newspapers. Orders started to trickle in, which was fine with Diane. She preferred to start slowly and let the business build gradually.

That was about three years ago. Helped by word-of-mouth advertising, she had added about $600 to her monthly income. This is just one way to start a side business in collectibles. It involves some work, but requires little investment. There is even an additional long-term benefit that many people don't even consider: As others become interested in a particular collectible, its value increases. So interest your friends—and your profits will probably grow!

The most enjoyable part of having your own side business—aside from the money you can make—is the fact that you can do it on your own time, at your own pace, and right from your own home. You can expand the business as you see fit, and watch it grow.

Stamps

About a year ago, Joe was talking about error stamps with Frank, a business associate. Frank had a few error stamps he wanted to sell. Joe knew the potential value of the stamps and wasn't about to pass up a golden opportunity.

"Frank," he said, "if you sell those stamps at auction, it's going to cost you at least another 10 percent in seller's fees. Those stamps are worth about $5,500—but you won't see all of the money. Plus there's no guarantee you'll get the price you want. If you can wait a few weeks, I'm positive I can find a buyer for you. I only want 5 percent of the selling price—but *only* if I get the price you want."

Frank agreed to wait a month. Joe knew there was no risk involved. He called his local newspaper and placed a classified ad under the heading "Unique Opportunity. Rare Stamps for Sale."

About three days after the ad appeared, Joe got a phone call from an interested buyer. Joe explained to the buyer exactly what he had. "You know," Joe said, "if you try to buy these stamps at auction, you'll have to pay the auction house at least a 10 percent buyer's fee. Plus, there's no guarantee you can get them for this price. All I want is 5 percent of the selling price, and I can guarantee you the stamps."

About a week later, after some haggling over price, Joe walked away with two checks—each for $290—$580 for a small amount of work. Not too bad.

And that was just the beginning. Joe began placing ads in local newspapers, some looking for buyers, the others looking for sellers. By bringing the two parties together and acting as a broker, Joe continued to make some nice extra money for himself.

People who wanted to buy these stamps appreciated Joe's efforts because he could guarantee them the stamps they wanted and save them the buyer's fee too. Sellers were happy because Joe guaranteed the price they wanted—otherwise he didn't get a commission. That one conversation with Frank gave Joe a whole new side business—and some much-needed extra cash.

Many people own stamps, but don't have the time or patience to buy and sell on their own. By acting as a stamp broker, you too can provide a worthwhile service.

All you need to start is a few small classified ads describing your service and a knowledge of stamp prices. You receive a commission only when you're successful, but you can take on as many clients as you want—and spend as much time as you desire.

Whatever you do, don't let the seller and the buyer get together, or even know who the other one is. You risk getting squeezed out of a rightfully earned commission if you do.

Building Your Own Stamp Business

Earlier you learned that stamps, particularly color-missing error stamps, are rising in value faster than almost any other collectible. Why?

- Because the supply is extremely limited
- Because interest is growing dramatically
- Because no more ever can be printed

You can, of course, make money by purchasing color-missing stamps for yourself and waiting for them to appreciate. You may, however, be able to make more money by obtaining them for other people.

Let's examine what you should do, step by step.

Obtain Some of These
Stamps for Yourself

Acquire some of the rare error stamps that Alan Shawn Feinstein recommends. Get them wherever you can, at the lowest possible price. The auction houses listed here are probably your best bet.

Watch for the Latest
Realized Auction Prices

After any auction, the auction house prints a list of "realized prices"—prices paid for each stamp sold at the most recent auction. These will keep you up to date on the current value of these stamps.

The two major auctions in this field are:

Jacques Schiff, Inc.
195 Main Street
Ridgefield Park, NJ 07660

Suburban Stamp Co.
1071 St. James Avenue
Springfield, MA 01104

They hold regular auctions about every six weeks. You can obtain auction prices by writing to them; better still, send $1.50 for the catalogs of their next auctions as well as their prices realized afterwards. Also, *The U.S. Error Stamp Club Newsletter* can keep you updated on these prices and provide valuable information. For a free sample copy, write Greg Hossler, Director, P.O. Box 645, Wilmington, MA 01887.

Obtain Some
Stamp Catalogs

The two major stamp catalogs that you should have are *The Minkus Stamp Catalog* and *The Scott Stamp Catalog*.

Prices in the Minkus catalog usually reflect stamps' retail values. The Scott prices are usually wholesale values.

You can use the catalog values as a basis for your own selling price. Keep in mind, however, that the prices for color-missing stamps are increasing with almost every auction. That's why it's also important to keep on top of the latest auction prices.

Show Your Stamps
to Friends and Neighbors

The stamps you already own can help you build your business. Show them to other people and explain their potential value. You may even want to draw up some charts showing how rapidly they are increasing in value.

If someone shows an interest in these stamps, explain how you can obtain them at a great savings. Don't forget to mention the 10 percent buyer's fee they would have to pay the auction house on top of the actual selling price. Remember to explain how competitive bidding at auctions can drive up the price of a stamp to a level much higher than its actual value.

Place Ads
in Local Newspapers

An ad with the headline, "Unique rare stamps. Outstanding appreciation potential," may put you in touch with investors who are interested in buying. Explain to these people how you can obtain stamps for them at a savings.

Contact Dealers
in Your Area

Ask the dealers in your area to put you in touch with anyone interested in buying or selling rare error stamps. Offer the dealer a small commission on any realized sale. Remember, many dealers still do not buy or sell error stamps. They may, however, know people who are interested in them, and they can be very helpful.

Buying Stamps
for Your Customers

Always get stamps for the lowest possible prices, not only when you buy for yourself, but also when you purchase them for others.

Check with wholesalers in your area after you get some orders. Wholesale prices are usually about 20 percent lower than the auction prices.

Pricing the Items You Sell

Attempt to sell at a level below the Minkus retail price, depending on the wholesale price you pay and the profit margin you want. In the beginning, it may be advantageous to offer larger discounts in an effort to get repeat business.

Guarantees

Offer the same type of guarantee that you would expect from any other stamp dealer—money back after ten days if the customer isn't completely satisfied.

Encourage your customers to get second and third opinions on everything you sell them. Their respect for you will grow when they see that the stamps are everything you say they are.

Watching Your
Business Grow

Sometimes word-of-mouth advertising is better than any print advertising you can buy. Your customers will show these stamps to their friends and neighbors, who may then want to buy some too. And where will they go? To you, of course.

Selling Collections
to Dealers

You can also act as a broker between sellers and dealers. Speak with dealers in your area and find out if they are interested in obtaining any stamp collections. Also find out if they will give you a 10 percent finder's fee on collections you obtain. Then place ads in local papers—directed at people interested in selling their collections. And remember, most dealers can't be bothered with small collections. Anything you obtain for them should be worth at least several hundred dollars.

A North Carolina woman who subscribes to the *Insiders Report* recently wrote to Alan Shawn Feinstein to tell him of a marvelous opportunity she uncovered, quite by accident. Ms. Stephenson (not her real name) purchased some demonetized bank notes recommended by Alan. She showed them to a few friends who, impressed by their artistic beauty but unaware of their potential value, wanted to know how to obtain some.

Though she didn't realize it at the time, Ms. Stephenson was about to become a collectibles dealer. She got the bank notes her friends wanted at wholesale, gave them a 10 percent discount off their retail price, and made a nice profit for herself.

Within the next month or so, she received four phone calls from people who saw the bank notes she had acquired for friends. They wanted some, too! What began as a favor blossomed into a business. With some of her profits, Ms. Stephenson advertised her "dealership" in area newspapers. She now has a steady clientele.

Alan encourages this as a way to make some extra money while introducing people to a great new collectibles field. And, although the field of foreign bank note collecting is very new, thanks to Alan and others who share his feelings, it is beginning to attract more and more collectors. Why?

- Demonetized bank notes are beautiful works of art, each with its own historical tale to tell
- Demonetized bank notes are still greatly undervalued, because people do not see their potential
- No more of these paper treasures will ever be printed

So while demand may increase (and we believe it will) the supply can only diminish, and you can profit from this growing field by becoming a bank note dealer. As you know, many coin and stamp dealers still don't, or won't, handle them. That's where you can come in.

The Advantage
of Bank Notes

One nice thing about demonetized bank notes is their price. Many can still be obtained for just a few dollars. It makes them affordable to people awed by the high prices of stamps, gems, and other collectibles. The best way to display their beauty to friends and neighbors is to purchase some for yourself. Obtain a representative sample—at the lowest possible price—of those Alan recommends.

Bank notes bought at wholesale are generally 30 to 40 percent off the retail price. By offering your customers a 10 percent discount off the retail price, you encourage people to buy more—and still make a fine profit.

Guarantees

Always give your customers an unconditional ten-day money-back guarantee. It builds confidence and good will. And, of course, always stand behind your guarantee if the request for a refund is reasonable.

Making Your Packages More Attractive

There are some things you can do to make the demonetized bank notes you sell more attractive.

1. Package your orders in small glassine envelopes or acetate currency holders, which you can purchase at any stamp store.

2. Write descriptive inserts for each of the bank notes. You can probably get this information from the library or other dealers. You should include information about the age of the bill, why it was taken out of circulation, and any interesting historical information. These inserts will make the demonetized bank notes even more enjoyable for the customers who purchase them.

3. Purchase some inexpensive business cards and include them in your packages. Word of mouth is a sure way to help your business grow.

With very little effort, your bank note business can grow into a very profitable operation.

Expanding Your Bank Note Business

1. Ask all of your customers for referrals, friends, or business acquaintances whom they think might be interested in bank notes. Then, if you have any printed materials, you can send them to referrals with a note saying, "Mr. _____ thought you might be interested in this." A recommendation from a satisfied customer can create many new opportunities to expand your business.

2. Advertise in local newspapers. A headline like "Rare demonetized bank notes for sale" may attract people who have never heard of these paper treasures. You can bring them into the field and get an entirely new stable of customers.

3. Attempt to start a bank note collectors' club and act as the organization's buyer and advisor. Again, a classified ad offering free details may attract some people to this rapidly growing field.

4. Keep up with current retail values by contacting dealers to find out what they're charging. You can use this information to demonstrate how bank notes are growing in value—and to show prospective buyers how much you can save them.

5. Offer your bank notes to gift and souvenir stores in your area. Although the retail market for bank notes is quite small, an enterprising businessperson—with your help—could make it larger. Many of Alan's subscribers are already doing this, making good profits.

Building Your Own
Autograph Business

Presidential autographs and signed documents are becoming extremely popular, yet many people don't know that such documents are available or where to get them. That's how you can help.

Presidential autographs are quite expensive. But there is a way that you can start an autograph business without buying or selling them yourself. By acting as a broker, you can spend your customers' money on autographs that they want. You can save them the auction fees and take a small commission on any realized sales.

The best way to approach this is by placing classified ads in local newspapers and collectors' publications. This will help you establish a list of individuals interested in obtaining these documents.

In the ads, ask people to request autographs that they are most interested in acquiring. You can then approach all of the dealers in your area—and even some out of your area— and get them. See Chapter 6 for a list of collectors' publications in which you can place your advertisements.

You can also act as a broker for prospective sellers. There are many museums, historical societies, and universities that are interested in acquiring signed presidential autographs and documents. Many autograph collectors sell their documents in this manner.

Here is a final idea. If you are imaginative and creative, you might interest finer gift and specialty shops in buying autographs. You can obtain a photograph of the president whose autograph you have, frame the picture and the document, and sell both. It might be a very attractive product for a store that specializes in unique items.

11

*Publications
No Collector
Should Be Without*

A smart collector is someone who gets as much information as possible before spending any money. We highly recommend you do the same.

There are many authoritative sources available in the area of collectibles. These magazines, organizational newsletters, books, and government documents will better prepare you for whatever venture you are about to enter.

Organizational Publications

Collectors' organizations should be a valuable source of information. They have the experience you lack and information you need. They may even be able to put you in touch with members who live in your area—people whom you can contact for information and advice.

Private Newsletters

Private newsletters can be very helpful or they can be absolutely worthless. It depends on the publication and who is putting it out. Because they provide "exclusive" information, subscription rates are sometimes very expensive.

Collectors' Magazines

Collectors' magazines may provide you with the most useful information. They are intended for all types of collectors, from the fledgling beginner to the hardened veteran. In addition, many dealers, wholesalers, and collectors advertise in these publications. They can be good sources for purchasing and selling.

Books

Your local library probably has hundreds of books about collectibles. These books can give you the most basic information you need to get started. Talk with the librarian about the subjects that most interest you. He or she should be able to direct you to useful books.

Government Documents

The United States Government Printing Office has a comprehensive list of publications, some of which may be helpful to you. Many of these publications are free; others are available for a nominal charge. You can obtain a complete list of these publications by writing:

Superintendent of Documents
United States Government Printing Office
Washington, D.C. 20402

Another government agency that will have information about stamps is the U.S. Postal Service. You may be able to obtain this information by simply contacting your local post office. If it doesn't have the literature on hand, it should be able to direct you to the correct agency.

Other Sources of Information

Recent issues of general magazines may also contain articles of interest to the collector. You can find this out by looking through the *Reader's Guide to Periodical Literature,* available at your local library. It carries an index of magazine articles on a variety of subjects, with the name of the magazine, issue, and page number. If you've never used the *Reader's Guide* before, your librarian can show you how.

Newspaper articles may also be a valuable source. Most libraries have some newspapers on microfilm, and almost every library has *The New York Times. The New York Times* index lists many of the articles that appeared in the newspaper, along with the date and page number. Your librarian can show you how to use both the index and the microfilm.

If your library doesn't store old newspapers on microfilm, there are other ways to get the information. Most major newspapers have their own libraries, and you can usually call to get information about articles.

Using the Information Wisely

Knowledgeable dealers and other collectors may be able to save you the trouble of looking through inferior publications, and they may also have some of the better publications to lend you.

When you talk with a dealer, ask him to put you in touch with some of his more experienced customers. These people should be more than willing to help you out. After all, they probably had to do the same thing when they started collecting.

Ultimately, only you can judge whether or not a publication can help you. There is so much information available that it's very easy to become confused about what's right and what isn't. If you aren't sure, ask someone whose advice you trust. In the end, though, always try to come to your own conclusions about the worth of any information you receive. It will make you a wiser collector.

Here is a list of publications worth inquiring about:

American Collector
100 E. San Antonio Street
Kermit, TX 78745

American Philatelic Services
 Report
Box 57
Lewiston, NY 14092

American Philatelist
American Philatelic Society
P.O. Box 800
State College, PA 16801

The Belleek Collector's
 Newsletter
Antigua 4, Box 371
La Mesa, CA 92041

Coin Collector Reporter
Box 1778
Fargo, ND 58102

Coin Collector and Shopper
Iola, WI 54945

Coin Market
Iola, WI 54945

Coin Prices
Iola, WI 54945

Coinage
17337 Ventura Blvd.
Encino, CA 91316

Coins
Iola, WI 54945

Collectors Club Philatelist
Collectors Club
22 East 35th Street
New York, NY 10016

The Confidential Report
P.O. Box 2727
New Orleans, LA 70176

Gem Market Reporter
P.O. Box 1469
Phoenix, AZ 85001

Gems and Gemology
Gemological Institute of
 America
1660 Stewart Street
Santa Monica, CA 90404

Gemstone Finance
Suite 1404
29 East Madison
Chicago, IL 60602

Gold Coin Newsletter
133 East 58th Street
New York, NY 10022

Guilds/American Gem Society
2960 Wilshire Blvd.
Los Angeles, CA 90010

International Banknote Society
P.O. Box 1222
Racine, WI 53405

Lapidary Journal
P.O. Box 80937
San Diego, CA 92138

Linn's Stamp News
P.O. Box 29
Sidney, OH 45367

Manuscripts
Morris Library
Southern Illinois University
Carbondale, IL 62901

Manuscripts
Manuscript Society
350 N. Niagara Street
Burbank, CA 91505

Mekeel's Stamp News
Box 1660
Portland, ME 04104

Minkus Stamp and Coin
Journal
116 West 32nd Street
New York, NY 10001

Numismatic Literature
American Numismatic Society
Broadway at 155th Street
New York, NY 10032

Numismatic News
Iola, WI 54945

Numismatic Scrapbook
P.O. Box 150
Sidney, OH 45365

Numismatics International
P.O. Box 30013
Dallas, TX 75230

The Numismatist
P.O. Box 2366
Colorado Springs, CO 80901

Paper Americana
P.O. Box 334
Baldwin Park, CA 91706

Paper Money
Society of Paper Money
Collectors
P.O. Box 3666
Cranston, RI 02910

The Pen and Quill
P.O. Box 467
Rockville Centre, NY 11571

Philatelic Foundation Newsletter
270 Madison Avenue
New York, NY 10016

Philatelic Guild's Investment
Newsletter
Box 798
Lakewood, NJ 08701

Rock and Gem
17337 Ventura Blvd.
Encino, CA 91316

Scott Stamp Market Update
3 East 57th Street
New York, NY 10022

Sotheby Parke Bernet
Newsletter
980 Madison Avenue
New York, NY 10021

Stamp Collector
Box 706
Albany, OR 97321

Stamp Exchanger's Annual
  Directory
P.O. Box 175
Irvington, NJ 07111

Stamp Trade International
1839 Palmer Avenue
Larchmont, NY 10536

The Stamper
3230 West 194th Street
Homewood, IL 60430

Stamps
153 Waverly Place
New York, NY 10014

Strictly U.S.
Dunedin, FL 33528

U.S. Error Stamp Club Newsletter
P.O. Box 645
Wilmington, MA 01887

World Coins
P.O. Box 150
Sidney, OH 45365

12

A Look
into the Future

What will the dollar be worth ten years from today? Will the seemingly never-ending cycle of high inflation and recession continue? What will happen to our economy as the world depletes its energy supply? Will you be able to retire comfortably when the time comes to do so?

These are questions that most of us—indeed, all of us—would like answered. Unfortunately, there probably aren't any definitive answers. If you were to put ten economists in the same room and asked them the same question, you'd probably get 15 different opinions. There are no crystal balls, no magic formulas that predict the future. There are just too many contingencies that can affect our economy. So how can you protect yourself—and your money—from the ravages of inflation?

You can acquire assets that are likely to withstand inflation—assets that will maintain their value even as paper money becomes worth less and less. You can acquire them *now*, when the price and demand are low and the supply is likely to decrease. And you can hold on to them and wait for the demand and price to increase.

Measuring Your Assets

How can you tell if a collectible can survive the economic roller coaster we've become accustomed to? Use these four characteristics to measure the value of what you own:

- Durability
- Convertibility
- Portability
- Tax Treatment

Durability. Can what you own keep pace with and outdistance inflation. You know, of course, that $100 today is no longer worth $100 in 1970 dollars.

Traditional savings accounts can't keep pace with inflation when the prevailing interest rates are 6 percent and inflation runs higher. Certificates of deposit and money market funds bring higher yields, but they also require larger deposits. With many of these investments, your money is tied up for a considerable period of time. Only tangible assets—not money—can be expected to stay with and beat inflation.

Convertibility. How well can you convert one asset to another without a loss of value? How easily can you sell it without losing money?

Let's use an automobile as an example. Six years ago you purchased a car for $6,000. Assuming it is in good condition, it might be worth half the purchase price on today's market. If you sell it, however, you must buy another one. And today, that same car probably costs $9,000. So you have really gained nothing.

Stamps, gems, and other collectibles are increasing in value. More people are trying to outdistance inflation by purchasing these items. Demand is increasing and there is a ready market for resale.

Portability. Can you take your assets with you? You can't strap a house on your back if you have to move. Gems, stamps, coins, and other collectibles have an international market, and can be bought and sold almost anywhere in the world.

Tax Treatment. How much of what you own is truly yours? How much belongs to the government? Taxes take a large bite out of your income. If you hold any collectible for more than one year and sell it for a profit (this also applies to homes, stocks, and real estate, by the way), you must pay a long-term capital gains tax.

It works like this. Only 40 percent of the capital gain is taxable and the tax you pay depends on the bracket you're in. Say, for example, you purchase a rare stamp for $1,000. Three years later, you sell it for $3,000. The capital gain is $2,000, 40 percent of which ($800) is taxable. If you are in the 30 percent bracket, the capital gains tax would be $240, 30% of the $800.

The tax laws that went into effect in January 1982 benefit only those people in the 50 to 70 percent tax bracket. There are two reasons for this: (1) the maximum tax on unearned income, formerly 70 percent, has been reduced to 50 percent; (2) the maximum capital gains tax has been reduced from 28 percent to 20 percent. If you are in a tax bracket of less than 50 percent, the same rules apply as before.

If the purpose behind your acquisition of collectibles is making a profit, you may be able to deduct expenses and losses. Say, for example, you need to raise cash to buy a rare and expensive stamp. If you sell other stamps at a loss to get this money, you may be able to deduct the losses you incurred.

Don't buy collectibles for investment solely for their tax advantages. Potential profits should always outweigh the taxes involved. Above all, speak to an accountant before considering any investment for tax purposes.

How the Economy
Affects Collectors

Two great economic problems of the past few years have been inflation and recession. If you are a collector, each will have an effect on you. During a recession, people are more likely to hold on to the cash they have and buy fewer collectibles. During recessionary periods, the collectibles market thus becomes a buyer's market.

Do not sell tangible assets during a recession; that's the time to buy. During periods of tight money, many people need cash and are willing to sell at sacrifice prices to get it.

People are more likely to buy collectibles during periods of high inflation. Their money is worth less and they want to protect themselves. With more people in the market to buy, prices are likely to rise.

How then can you cope with high inflation? Do not buy tangible assets during an inflationary period, one in which inflation is higher than 10 percent.

Collectibles are not immune to dips in value. During periods of recession and tight money, many collectibles drop in value, as do other things—although, as a rule, not as much. During such times, the wise collector knows he should never sell. Instead, he should hold on until inflation surges—until values rise again—usually at a rate higher than inflation. Signs of a coming recession or rising inflation may help you make important decisions about buying and selling.

Collectibles and
"Instant" Liquidation

Many people who buy collectibles think they can buy one day, sell the next, and still make a nice profit. It is possible, but collectibles really are not effective vehicles for quick sales and quick profits.

Some people see this lack of "instant liquidity" as a reason not to buy collectibles. On the contrary, the lack of instant liquidity may be one reason why collectibles buyers rarely suffer the losses that people involved in stocks, options, and commodities futures do.

Whenever there's bad news, many people get the urge to sell their stock. There's a sudden influx of "sell" orders and not enough buyers. Most sellers can't get the price they want. People who hold futures or options can suffer horrendous losses waiting for the execution of a sell order.

Buyers of collectibles, on the other hand, are not likely to surrender at the slightest hint of bad news. They wait for the best and are much more likely to search and wait for a fair price.

So don't expect to get instant cash if you buy collectibles. They will most likely go up in value, but the larger rewards will come to those who wait.

World Politics
and Collectibles

Of the collectibles that Alan Shawn Feinstein recommends, only gems are affected by the politics of other nations. The effect, however, can be a positive one for those who already own colored gems.

As the OPEC nations have discovered with oil, natural resources can be used to increase the amount of hard currency a country takes in. Nations with large gemstone deposits are slowly discovering this. In the future, many developing nations may try to limit the amount of gems they export. For the collector, this means a likely increase in the value of gems already on the market. Brazil, for example, has passed laws restricting the numbers of gems that can be exported to foreign nations. In Thailand large supplies of rubies are found in the border areas near Cambodia and Laos—a part of the world that is politically unstable. These deposits could be taken by the Communists, or the present Thai government, fearful of depleting a major resource, could cut or cease production and exports. Emeralds are mined primarily in Colombia and Africa, two areas of the world not known for their political stability.

What the Future Holds

Economic upheavals such as inflation and recession are almost certain to continue, since no one seems to be able to bring these problems under control. To protect yourself and the value of your savings in this ever-changing world, remember: Search out items that are in limited supply and growing demand and buy them wherever you can at the lowest prices.

Above all, remember the treasures of Alan Shawn Feinstein. Even if you do nothing more, watch carefully what happens to their values in the days ahead. (An easy way to do this is to write to Alan for a free copy of his *International Insiders Report,* Box 2065, Dept. B., Cranston, RI 02905.) I think you will be astonished.

Index

A

Alan Shawn Feinstein & Associates, 58
ALS, 69, 70
Amber, 43
American Collectibles, 68, 71, 80
American Philatelic Services Report (periodical), 17
American Philatelic Society (APS), 95
Amethyst, 44
Antique and Collectors Mart (periodical), 16–17
Appraisal of gems, 46, 47
Approval purchasing, 98, 99, 107
Aquamarine, 39, 40, 44
Auction houses:
  autographs, 71, 78–79
  bidding, 29, 86, 107–8
  buying through, 26–30, 33, 71, 86, 107–9
  danger of fraud and, 94–95, 99
  error stamps, 26–29, 31, 33, 118
  "realized price" lists from, 118
  selling through, 31, 61, 78–79, 110–12
Authenticity, certificates of, 71, 95, 96, 99, 105
Autographed letters (ALS), 69, 70
Autographs, *see* Presidential autographs

B

Bank notes, demonetized, 17–18, 51–63, 85
  buying, 57–58
  care of, 60
  condition of, 58–59
  conservation of, as business venture, 115
  counterfeit, 60, 96
  current retail values of, 56–57
  descriptions of, 51–56
  information sources on, 57–58, 132, 133
  selling, 60–62
  starting own business in, 121–23
Baseball cards, 61–62, 83–87
Beatles, the, 83, 87
Bidding, 29, 86, 107–8
Bonds, 15, 16, 84
Boston University, 18
Burglary protection, 18
Buyer's commissions, 108, 110–11
Buying:
  through auctions, 26–30, 33, 71, 86, 107–9
  from dealers, 26, 34, 57–58, 71–73, 103–7, 112
  demonetized bank notes, 57–58
  error stamps, 26–30, 34–35, 118–20
  gems, 43–48, 107–8

143